'A fascinating and insightful j...
stories of characters in the Bi...
and others' lives today. This...
stimulate the mind, touch ...
ment with the human stories ...people, past and present.'

'*Finding Our Voice* will be a great help for those who are trying to find words, who long to be heard and for those who want to listen more carefully.'

'Full of humanity and grace, *Finding Our Voice* is honest and challenging and painful. Yet, it is also shot through with the mercy and grace of God in a way which will deepen faith and give birth to new hope.'

'*Finding Our Voice* gives voice to some of the anonymous characters of Scripture, but also gives fresh voice and significance to contemporary stories of pain.'

'I love the way this book opens our eyes to new characters of the Bible interwoven with some up-to-date stories that will assist new and experienced readers alike to become more aware of God's Word, seeing it in a new light.'

Dave Lock, Manager, Manna Christian Centre Christian Bookshop; and chairman, Christian Booksellers Group for the Booksellers Association in Great Britain & Ireland

'This is a wonderfully accessible yet thought-provoking and enriching book. Jeannie uses her great story-telling skills to bring the stories of unnamed yet important characters from the Bible to life by giving them a voice. She then gives additional context, before allowing contemporary people their voice, which creates resonance with the biblical characters for us all.'

Julie Aylward, prison chaplain

'This is an important book. Jeannie has brought Bible stories to life with a new energy, and the contemporary stories that she shares show how devastatingly powerful biblical truth is for today.'

Revd Jonathan Edwards, former General Secretary of the Baptist Union, adviser to Torch Trust and Through the Roof, advocate for Parish Nursing Ministries UK and an ambassador for Premier Media

'Combined with unobtrusively scholarly interpretation, Jeannie Kendall brings the Bible into contemporary life in a way that engages the emotions and sparks application to our own and our neighbours' lives wherever we live, whatever our age or background.'

Dr Rachel Johnson, former Research Librarian, University of Worcester, currently working at Tyndale House, Cambridge and introduced through helpfully descriptive chapter headings allowing the reader to choose areas of special interest.'

Deborah Haythorne, CEO, Roundabout; dramatherapist and supervisor www.roundaboutdramatherapy.org.uk

'A remarkable book . . . *Finding Our Voice* shows us, with heartbreak and hope, voices that remind us of our common humanity, that draw us to the God who hears each of us and, quite simply, will not let us go.'

Revd Joseph Haward, author, founder of the educational resource site revdjoe.com, pioneer pastor and community chaplain

'I was moved and challenged, but was aware throughout of God's love and tender mercy for all of us, whatever our circumstances.'

Cedric Pierce, former professional in the criminal justice system

'I hope the book enables Christians and non-Christians to hear their own stories through the variety of subjects she has chosen and realise the impact the grace and love of God can have and has on our lives.'

Linda Campbell, Director of Practical Training and Admissions, Spurgeons College

'If you are looking for a fresh way to read and consider biblical stories, as well as contemplating your own, then I can heartily recommend this book to you.'

Claire Musters, speaker, writer and editor

'The Bible's brief portraits of unnamed, seemingly insignificant, hurt and damaged people come alive in Jeannie's hands. Through all the brokenness we can trace a thread of hope that leads us back to the heart of God.'

Paul Tyas, musician and fellow-traveller

'All the stories told here are worth listening to, and by allowing them to have an impact there is the possibility of finding God's story interwoven with our own.'

Ruth Dormandy, pastoral psychotherapist, supervisor, consultant and trainer

'A gift of genuine healing aides and a guide for individual or group Bible study.'

R. W. White, author and retired clergy: URC (UK) & PC (USA)

'Challenging, moving and uplifting . . . The biblical and present-day stories throw light on important life issues through different layers and lenses.'

Rosanne Tyas, professional lead, music therapy, Royal Hospital for Neuro-disability

'*Finding Our Voice* is a beautiful collection of biblical interpretations alongside true stories of loss and redemption. The mirroring of the Bible alongside real-life stories creates a depth and unique perspective on these biblical truths and their ultimate relevance to our lives today.'

Dr Ann-Marie Wilson, Founder & Executive Director, 28 Too Many

'Dealing with a wide spectrum of human life, this book is both light and deep, and full of wisdom.'
Andy Percey, author and minister, Manvers Street Baptist Church

'Jeannie creates a tripartite story structure where the personal experiences of present-day contributors sit alongside the original and retold Bible stories linked through common themes

Finding Our Voice

Unsung lives from the Bible resonating with stories from today

Jeannie Kendall

To mike and marie,
Such faithful servants of our
wonderful Lord,
   May God encourage you as
you read,
                Jeanie
                  July 2019
                  Zx

Authentic

First published 2019 by Authentic Media Limited,
PO Box 6326, Bletchley, Milton Keynes, MK1 9GG
authenticmedia.co.uk

British Library Cataloguing in Publication Data
A catalogue record for this book is available from the British Library.
ISBN: 978-1-78893-037-6
978-1-78893-038-3 (e-book)

Cover design by Vivian Hansen
Printed and bound by CPI Group (UK) Ltd., Croydon, CR0 4YY

Contents

Foreword   xi

Introduction   1
Part 1 Journeys   **5**
  1 Leaving Home   7
  2 Living with Depression   22
  3 Searching for Meaning   35
  4 The Impact of Forgiveness   50
  5 Discovering Love   63
Part 2 Challenges   **75**
  6 Losing a Child   77
  7 Overcoming Shame   89
  8 Facing Long-term Illness   101
  9 Surviving Abuse   114
 10 Confronting Death   126
 11 Finding Hope   137

Final Reflections   151
Acknowledgements   155
Notes   159
Bibliography   169
Websites   173
Scripture/Story Index   175

This book is dedicated to several groups of people.

First of all, to all the courageous people who have allowed me to tell their stories – I only hope I have done them justice.

Secondly, to those many people who have helped me find my own voice: you know who you are, but particularly to my friend and colleague Phil Hornsey and the church family at Beeches Baptist church.

Above all it is dedicated to my precious family: Malcolm, Amy and Vali, Faith and Gabriel and Ross and Helen. My story has been enriched by you all beyond measure.

Foreword

If making the Scriptures sing in the language of today is one of the preacher's gifts, then Jeannie Kendall sings sweet and true in this book. These are not sermons, but the preacher in Jeannie is unmistakeable. The Scriptures sing here in a way very reminiscent of Ignatian scriptural contemplation, and with all of the richly imaginative art of retelling the story on display. And if understanding people in all of their heartache and possibilities for transformation lies at the heart of pastoral ministry, then this book is a sustained piece of pastoral theology in a narrative register that will ring true for many.

I am not surprised that Jeannie Kendall in undertaking this task has produced such rich results, for she is a fine preacher and amongst the most accomplished pastors I know. This is, therefore, the fruit of half a lifetime of pastoral ministry from one who has been first a gifted pastoral counsellor and trainer of others, and more recently a faithful and effective pastor in the Baptist tradition – in which capacity she still serves a local congregation.

In my first pastorate, Jeannie and I served together at 'Lewin Road', as Streatham Baptist Church was fondly known. Instrumental in establishing Manna Counselling Service above the Christian bookshop and café on Streatham High Road, Manna

Christian Centre, Jeannie was at the heart of that ministry. When the call to ordained ministry came to her, Jeannie transferred from counsellor to associate pastor at the same church while being formed nearby at theological college. I had by this time moved to another church, but I would hear reports of the wise and sensible ministry she offered, when others dabbled in the 'wacky', and at its heart was her godly pastoral ministry – 'professional' in all of the best ways, and with none of the indifference or poverty of commitment that can bring the 'p'-word ('professional') into such disrepute. The members of her current church were wise enough to call her, and there she continues to offer the best of pastoral ministry.

Jeannie is also a poet, and her literary gifts are used to the full in this book, creating a flow in the text that makes you want to come back for more of these elegant and deeply felt narratives. Where some, mistakenly, want the Christian Scriptures to be merely a mine to be quarried for propositional nuggets about God, the world and the godly life, Jeannie in these weavings of scriptural narrative, its imaginative retelling and the stories of others, shows how at their heart, the books of the Bible tell stories that invite our participation in God's great story. His story, becoming history, becomes our story too. In her retelling of God's story, we too can enter into the ways in which the Christian faith is resistant to easy answers to life's most challenging questions, or is susceptible to the need to tie up every loose end in a neat and packaged consumer product. These stories are lived in the raw, as they should be, and are the faithful response to that poetic and theological weaving.

Revd Dr Paul Goodliff is a Baptist minister and pastoral theologian currently serving as General Secretary of Churches Together in England.

Introduction

Storytelling is the most effective and cross-cultural form of human communication.[1]

Nigel Wright

Stories are important. From early childhood we are (hopefully) told stories, and the imagination of many children is peopled with characters from those stories as we grapple to make sense of the world. These narratives become intermingled with the story we write of our own lives. We may see ourselves as princes or princesses, as heroes who need to rescue others, or find our lives blighted by others designating us as villains, particularly if we then believe these negative characterisations and live them out. Those stories we tell ourselves about our lives become part of our internal world and are crucial to how we see ourselves and to our emotional wellbeing.

This book and its origin has its own story. I can remember the exact moment it began to unfold, though no doubt it was (to change the metaphor) growing within me long before that. Pondering what I should do with an upcoming sabbatical, I was surprised when several people – unaware I was looking to take time out – asked me if I had ever thought about writing a book. I simply laughed. Although I love words and stories, and have always written in different ways, it seemed an impossible dream.

A month or so later, on holiday, I sat in companionable silence with my husband on a clifftop on Jersey. As I watched the gulls wheeling and allowed my often frenzied thoughts to be soothed by the rhythm of the waves, two thoughts fell into place with great clarity. The first was more a reminder, a prompt that for some years I had been fascinated with the unnamed characters in the Bible. In what ways did their stories have, somehow, even more power for us precisely because they were unnamed? What part might their story have in the grander narrative of God? And in what ways did they resonate with my own story and that of others? If they could find their voice in a new way, might we too?

The second was remembering that I have for a long time had a passion that people should find their own voice, tell their unique story with the assurance that it matters, and has significance. A friend later rightly remarked that this, above all, would give me the fire and persistence to continue with the lengthy process of bringing a book to birth. As a teacher, counsellor and then minister, I have been privileged to hear many people's stories and, I hope, helped give them confidence to tell them and have them heard and held safely.

At supper that Jersey evening, unaware of any of those thoughts, my husband said to me, most unexpectedly, 'As we sat there today I thought that you should write a book,' later explaining that he really believed that was from God, not just his own thoughts. So the idea for this book became clear and took on a life of its own.

Each chapter has a similar format, giving voice imaginatively to one of the unnamed characters of the Bible, followed by looking at the actual story in its context, and then telling a story on a similar theme from our own era. With the first part of each chapter I have tried to keep faithful to the biblical account, though at times I have filled in gaps in ways I do not believe conflict with it. The current stories are real and used with permission, with only minor changes to preserve confidentiality. Names are also omitted in these sections, in line with the anonymity of the biblical characters and also to free the reader to identify with what is written. Some of both the Bible stories and the modern ones make for tough reading – but that is the inescapable reality of our world.

My prayer is that this book will enable you to do at least three things. Firstly, whether you are new to it or have read it many times, to look at the Bible in a new way, as the extraordinarily current and relevant book that I believe it is, speaking into issues that are timeless and faced by every generation. Secondly, to find echoes of your own story which will give you confidence to own it, to speak – or sing or draw – it out in whatever way you choose, and see where you too may fit in the bigger tale of the master story-teller. Thirdly, to learn from stories that may be very different from your own – unfamiliar stories can also move, encourage and challenge us and help us to understand each other better.

It may be that you are drawn to some chapters more immediately than others, and they are all self-contained, so you can read them in any order that appeals to you. I would encourage you, however, in time, to read them all. Sometimes we can be surprised, and learn even more from the things to which we are not immediately attracted. Each chapter can be read alone, or shared in a group where you hear each other's voices too. Stories are by their very nature unique, and the modern stories are not an exact match of the biblical ones. They are not intended to be, but to draw on the same timeless themes.

However you read them, I pray that God meets you in these pages and you can hear, whether for the first time or again, his voice of encouragement and love for you, and know that your own story is known by and precious to him.

Part 1

Journeys

1

Leaving Home

*The foreigner residing among you must be
treated as your native-born. Love them as yourself, for you were foreigners in Egypt.*[1]

The Torah

Hearing a Voice from the Past

I was so frightened. War is so terrifying, and I was so young. I
could feel the panic all around me – my parents, who had been
my rock, were desperately trying to shield me from it, but I
could sense their anxiety and that of my whole village. We were
not allowed to play outside any more and I missed my friends.
There were no food treats as we were not sure what was going
to happen with our crops – whether they might be burned or
taken.

Then one day the very thing we had dreaded happened. Our
neighbours from Aram attacked our village again. The soldiers
came, harsh lines etched in their faces and determination in
their eyes. We hid in our house, hoping we might be over-
looked, but we were soon discovered. I can still see him now, a
huge figure silhouetted in the doorway by the dazzling midday

sun. He looked at us and then, as my mother screamed, lifted me up and carried me away. It was the last time I would ever see my village, or my land. Or, the hardest thing of all, my precious family.

I prayed to my God, the God of Israel, though I barely knew what to ask. From my earliest days my parents had told me that the God who looked after us was the God of the whole world and not just one tribe or nation, and that he sent people who spoke for him, like Elisha the prophet. I had heard stories about him. His father had been a farmer in the next village to ours, and it is said that the great prophet Elijah had found him there and called him to be his apprentice. Just recently we had heard stories of both things and people being healed by God through him – a poisonous spring and even a child. Some said the boy was raised from the dead, others that God had provided a widow with a miraculous supply of oil because of Elisha. I'd often really wished that I could meet him. I knew I never would now.

All these thoughts were flooding my mind as I was carried away, and I tried to think of them rather than the screams I heard and the acrid smoke from the many fires which burned my lungs and brought even more tears to my eyes. As night fell I became frightened as the journey continued. Where was I going? What was going to happen to me? Were my parents and my brother alright? I shivered with cold and fright and tried to be still so as not to make my captors angry.

Just as I thought the journey would never end, we stopped. I was exhausted from lack of sleep and worry, but warily I looked around me. We had stopped at a house: it was quite big, larger and grander than anything I had seen in my homeland, and I wondered whose it was. Inside I was taken to a lady who looked me over like my mother used to when she checked an item she was going to purchase at the market. But her eyes were not unkind. At first when she spoke to me, I could not understand her – she spoke Aramaic too, but in a very different accent and with some new words. We could manage well enough, though, and she made it clear that I was to look after her.

Those early days were so difficult. I cried in secret for my family. Nothing was familiar, and even trying to help my mistress was complicated because I did not understand how her clothing worked or how chores were done there or everything she said. At times I was furious with the war-makers and angry too with the God who I felt had done nothing to protect us. They worshipped idols there and I hated that. I tried to pray but always found myself weeping. I struggled to hold on to the stories of my people, like when Joseph was taken as a slave, but God turned it around in the end. But it was so very, very tough.

My mistress was gentle, though, and so, as time went on, I came to accept that I was there and had somehow to adapt to my new life. I still ached for the old one, and I still shed tears, but from being consumed by my own distress, I started to look around me and notice more.

I learned that my master, Naaman, was a very important man. He was commander of the army that had captured me. At first this made me resentful of him, though I had always to hide it. In the constant tug-of-war between our countries, he had been the one who led the army that, this last time, defeated us. He was not unkind, though he was a large and imposing man and I felt daunted by him if our paths ever crossed, so I kept out of his way.

A while after the war ended (at least I assumed it had, since he was at home all the time), I noticed a change in the atmosphere of the house. There was no more laughter, as there had been. My mistress looked red-eyed at times as though she had been crying. She didn't wear her special clothes any more because her husband stopped visiting her and stayed all the time in his own quarters. For a while I said nothing, and then one day I carefully asked if everything was alright. She looked at me, her eyes brimming with tears.

'No,' she said. 'He has leprosy.'

That one word was enough. I had seen lepers once, at a distance, hoods covering their faces, crying 'unclean' to make sure we did not come near. My parents had to explain, and so now I knew what that meant; all the isolation for fear of passing it on, the disfigurement and gradual loss of sensation and the prospect of dying away from your family. I could not bear to think of that as my master's future, even though his army had ripped me from my home and my old life. All my anger and resentment melted away as my heart went out to them both. I said nothing, as I knew I could not say anything that would help. Words felt inadequate and insensitive in the company of so much pain.

I prayed to my God. If anyone could help, surely he could. I remembered the story my mother had told me, after I had seen the lepers that day, of how he healed Moses and Miriam of leprosy. But no miracle came. Then one day, as I rose from prayer, I remembered the stories about Elisha. Maybe he could help, but how could I get my master to go? He was such a proud man. So I did the only thing I could, and told my mistress. She listened carefully as I told her all the stories about Elisha that I knew, and I could see the glimmer of hope in her eyes.

I heard nothing for a while, and then one day my master saddled his horse, and took his servants with many packages and rode off. My mistress drew me aside.

'He's going,' she whispered.

I could see her mix of excitement and fear – what if it was no good? What if he came back shattered by yet another disappointment? I felt that worry too.

I prayed and prayed to my God while he was gone, and then one day my master returned at last. I could see from his face, and from the way he ran to take my mistress in his arms, that he was well. They laughed, and cried, and I wept too.

Later I heard what had happened, but that is his story, not mine. But there was one change that was wonderful for me. He had brought back sacksful of earth from just near the Jordan, and he made a patch at the back of his house where he and his household could pray. He let me use it too. It was a little of my home in this foreign land and I thanked God.

My God cares for all people, even army commanders. And he cares for exiles and refugees. He cares for me.

***

The story is found in 2 Kings 5:1–19:

Now Naaman was commander of the army of the king of Aram. He was a great man in the sight of his master and highly regarded, because through him the LORD had given victory to Aram. He was a valiant soldier, but he had leprosy.

[2] Now bands of raiders from Aram had gone out and had taken captive a young girl from Israel, and she served Naaman's wife. [3] She said to her mistress, 'If only my master would see the prophet who is in Samaria! He would cure him of his leprosy.'

[4] Naaman went to his master and told him what the girl from Israel had said. [5] 'By all means, go,' the king of Aram replied. 'I will send a letter to the king of Israel.' So Naaman left, taking with him ten talents of silver, six thousand shekels of gold and ten sets of

clothing. [6] The letter that he took to the king of Israel read: 'With this letter I am sending my servant Naaman to you so that you may cure him of his leprosy.'

[7] As soon as the king of Israel read the letter, he tore his robes and said, 'Am I God? Can I kill and bring back to life? Why does this fellow send someone to me to be cured of his leprosy? See how he is trying to pick a quarrel with me!'

[8] When Elisha the man of God heard that the king of Israel had torn his robes, he sent him this message: 'Why have you torn your robes? Make the man come to me and he will know that there is a prophet in Israel.' [9] So Naaman went with his horses and chariots and stopped at the door of Elisha's house. [10] Elisha sent a messenger to say to him, 'Go, wash yourself seven times in the Jordan, and your flesh will be restored and you will be cleansed.'

[11] But Naaman went away angry and said, 'I thought that he would surely come out to me and stand and call on the name of the LORD his God, wave his hand over the spot and cure me of my leprosy. [12] Are not Abana and Pharpar, the rivers of Damascus, better than all the waters of Israel? Couldn't I wash in them and be cleansed?' So he turned and went off in a rage.

[13] Naaman's servants went to him and said, 'My father, if the prophet had told you to do some great thing, would you not have done it? How much more, then, when he tells you, "Wash and be cleansed"!' [14] So he went down and dipped himself in the Jordan seven times, as the man of God had told him, and his flesh was restored and became clean like that of a young boy.

[15] Then Naaman and all his attendants went back to the man of God. He stood before him and said, 'Now I know that there is no God in all the world except in Israel. So please accept a gift from your servant.'

[16] The prophet answered, 'As surely as the LORD lives, whom I serve, I will not accept a thing.' And even though Naaman urged him, he refused.

[17] 'If you will not,' said Naaman, 'please let me, your servant, be given as much earth as a pair of mules can carry, for your servant will never again make burnt offerings and sacrifices to any other god but the LORD. [18] But may the LORD forgive your servant for this one thing: when my master enters the temple of Rimmon to bow down and he is leaning on my arm and I have to bow there also – when I bow down in the temple of Rimmon, may the LORD forgive your servant for this.'

[19] 'Go in peace,' Elisha said.

For this story we leave the land of Israel, where most of both the Bible and this book are set, and step into Aram, now known as Syria, to the north. Naaman was a soldier, everything that represents strength. He was someone who would have been revered and respected, a captain, second in command to the king, and had been part of a Syrian victory over Israel when this unnamed young girl had been taken from her family. He was a man of great authority and position, at the pinnacle of his career. His name means 'be delightful, pleasant, beautiful' and has the idea of 'gracious' or 'well formed', which must have seemed a cruel irony when the illness struck. For some reason, out of all the captives, he has chosen this particular girl to serve his wife. We can only speculate what he saw in her to make that choice, whether her age, her looks, his perception of her personality, or a combination of them all.

Yet underneath all his celebrity there is a tragedy. He has a huge difficulty. He has leprosy, now called Hansen's disease.[2] There are actually two kinds of this disease, one always fatal and the other disfiguring but not life-threatening, but they were both dreaded because they were believed (falsely) to be highly contagious. Sufferers were separated from others in colonies: whenever they went out they had to cry, 'unclean, unclean', to wear black with a hood covering their faces and live outside the city walls. It was a disease which carried no hope. People would be anxious as soon as they got any skin blemish, because it might be the start of this particular feared disease.

We don't know from the Bible text when he first got this disease. If he had it for some time, how did he manage the illness as a soldier? Presumably he would have bound up his sores, both to keep from contaminating anyone but also perhaps because of how he felt about himself and his appearance. Whenever he contracted it, it would have been a terrible thing for him and his family. As a Jew (unlike the Syrians), it would have been forbidden under the purity laws for this girl to associate with a person with leprosy, but the sense we get from this story is that in wanting to see him healed she is motivated by concern for her captors rather than adhering to the rules of her faith.

His maid is a nobody in that society. She is a refugee, part of the spoils of war, a foreigner and a young girl – possibly even as young as 10 or 12. It would have been so easy to nurse her bitterness – this man was captain of the same army who captured her. Where was God in this situation? The implication of her story is that if she had become angry and bitter and so kept silent Naaman would have potentially been isolated from his family, his occupation, and perhaps died. She has mercy and compassion even though this man – or at least what he represented – had done her the most appalling damage. So she decides to tell his wife, her mistress, about the prophet Elisha.

Elisha was a prophet, a person who sought to speak for God,[3] who lived in the ninth century BC and whose story is told from 1 Kings 19 through to 2 Kings 13. It was a time of great religious activity. There were at least thirty prophets, at work in both the northern kingdom of Israel and the southern kingdom of Judah, challenging both nations to turn away from idolatry and other sins. Elisha had been chosen and discipled by Elijah, although in some ways their ministries were quite different, Elijah often being associated with stern confrontation.[4] Elisha was able to build on Elijah's work with a slightly gentler approach, including being associated with various miracles of healing.[5]

Although what happens next is not the servant girl's story, it is interesting. Naaman, presumably desperate enough to try anything, goes to the king of Syria, Ben-Hadad, with the news and to get permission to go to Israel. The king was willing to help,[6] but they both immediately think in terms of political and financial clout.[7] They assume they can buy the favours of God from the prophet of Yahweh through the king of Israel, Jehoram.[8] So Naaman is sent to the king of Israel rather than to the prophet Elisha, with a letter of commendation, taking a large amount of silver, gold and clothes as payment. This was the typical cultural pattern of that day but, as the story unfolds, it is clearly not God's way. Naaman sets off on the long journey thinking he can perhaps buy a cure.

Instead of immediately pointing Naaman to Elisha the prophet, Jehoram the king is paranoid and paralysed with fear. He knows he can't bring a cure and thinks that the king of Syria is seeking an excuse to create an incident and so a justification for another attack. Instead of seeing this visit as an opportunity to build relations or demonstrate the power of Israel's God, he is concerned for self-preservation. What a contrast to the unnamed slave girl who thought of others rather than her own plight.

It must have been a moment of some anxiety for Naaman when the king tore his robes, culturally a sign of grief or righteous indignation. Perhaps it shattered part of his trust in his own human resources. What he thought would buy his cure was worthless. What is there for him now? Where does it leave his search for a cure?

Fortunately Elisha hears about it, and sends for Naaman. This must have been a picture of real contrast: the Syrian army commander in his chariot with his pedigree horses, his gold and silver and fine clothes standing in front of the prophet's house, which was probably very unimpressive by Naaman's standards. We get the sense that Naaman is a proud man – confident in his accomplishments, talents, power, position and wealth. The implication of his anger in verse 11 is that he had ridden up arrogantly and expects this lowly prophet of Israel to come out to him, Naaman the great warrior and honoured guest, and wave his hand over the area of his leprosy in person to cure him. We see his pride and conceit, cultural as well as individual, expressing itself in various ways, perhaps unsurprisingly given the rivalry between the two nations. Especially we see it in his anger at being told to go and wash seven times in the Jordan, a river he considers vastly inferior to those in his homeland.

Elisha's actions could be viewed as unwelcoming, rude and arrogant. But what Elisha does appears to be a means of showing Naaman his pride so he could receive God's grace. Naaman initially reacts badly and snorts off. Elisha doesn't run after him; it seems he simply turned it over to the sovereignty of God who then worked through the lives of other unnamed servants to bring Naaman to his senses.

In the end, after a brave intervention from his own servants, Naaman decides he has nothing to lose, and continues on to the river. When he gets there he literally plunges in – having made the decision to try it, he is not half-hearted. And he is healed. It is interesting that Elisha refuses his gift, a sign of Naaman's profound gratitude, although the prophet earlier received help from the Shunammite woman. Perhaps Elisha wanted him to learn that God was not like other gods and did not need to be paid. He wants Naaman to rely less on his riches and begin to understand God's kindness.

Naaman's request to take the earth back to his home is interesting and the exact reason is not specified, only implied by his comments. He knows that he will have to return to his old environment and live in the midst of idolatry. We can surmise that the earth might be so that he might erect an altar to Yahweh on which he could offer sacrifices for a witness to the God of Israel in his own land, or as an evidence of his determination to forsake all other gods. Whatever the exact reason, Naaman is clearly concerned about worshipping the God he had newly discovered even though his duties will mean externally honouring other gods (see v. 18). Elisha's only response is, 'Go in peace,' implying his assurance that God understands. The issue as he returned to his homeland would be his attitude and heart, not soil or buildings.

All we know of this unnamed[9] girl's background is just twenty-three words and we have only one recorded remark from her, but the impact she had was hugely significant. We cannot help but wonder what happened to her after the healing. Might Naaman have sent her home in gratitude for his healing, or because she had become so important in their family life, would he have kept her there? We can only guess. It is so frustrating when we don't know the full ending of the story, but that is a reality that will be reflected many times in the subsequent chapters of this book. What we do know is that God used her to bless others, and he can use exiles and refugees in all kinds of ways. This same God, whose own son would one day be a refugee,[10] loves and cares for every one of them too, and knows every name and every story.

***

Hearing a Voice from the Present

I think, before it actually happened, it might have been hard
for me to imagine the impact of one young refugee girl. Yet she
has had the most profound effect on the direction of my life.

Let me start by setting the encounter in context. I had been
brought up attending church, but became a more committed
Christian following an Alpha course in 1999. After that I took
a three-month sabbatical to volunteer with the organisation
Medair.[11]

Those months were the first time I had ever seen that level
of deprivation. At first I was in a Kakuma refugee camp for
Sudanese refugees in Kenya as part of a team looking for volun-
teers to run education programmes. The war in the Sudan was
truly terrible, as all war is, but it did give an opportunity for
some of the people there to change their lives. They had come
from situations of abject poverty, but in the camps they had
food, albeit rationed, and education, and so there were some
signs of hope amid the suffering.

Later I moved to work in Kibera, in the centre of Nairobi
in Kenya. This informal housing settlement was not for those
from other countries, but those who had been displaced inter-
nally by losing their right to housing for a variety of reasons.
Often they had been moved from the land they had inhabited
because of changes in farming. It was a very big geographical
area – about five square kilometres, nearly two square miles,
about six and a half kilometres outside Nairobi itself. It was
the largest slum (a term I dislike intensely, but which gives the
feel of what it was like) in Africa. So many things assault your
senses – in particular the smell and the humiliating loss of dignity for the people there. There was a whole missing generation
due to deaths from HIV. Families were sleeping in bunk beds

in one-room buildings with tin roofs. Prostitution was rife as a means of somehow making some income when there was no hope of finding a way out. The enormity of the poverty and the sense of communal helplessness shocked me to the core.

By 2003 I was with Medair full-time and now working in Northern Sudan. It was there in West Darfur that I met a little girl who was to change the direction of my future. This young girl had been through the most unimaginable suffering. Already a victim of the practice of female genital mutilation,[12] she had been raped aged just 10 by armed militia and then left for dead, seven months pregnant. Aged 11 she was sent to be a forced wife. We hoped that there might be a way found for her to change her life, perhaps retraining elsewhere. This encounter broke my heart and gave me a renewed passion not just for people with such deprivation, but specifically for women who have encountered gender-based violence and FGM.

I went back to college, training in psychology with a speciality in gender-based violence, and as part of my training had a placement at the largest refugee camp in the world, Dadaab on the Somali-Kenya border. Numerically at one point it had reached half a million people – when I was there it numbered about quarter of a million. It was like a town in the middle of the desert, and 'housed' Somalian refugees, who were there as a result of the combination of drought and the ongoing civil war in Somalia.

Situations of such desperation birth so many tragic complexities. Sometimes children with disabilities were 'adopted' by other refugees to help increase their chances of repatriation in the West. Although it is so clearly right to provide water and sanitation, sometimes the wrong kind of aid can disrupt family structures as there is no need to work. Although this camp was for refugees, some residents were actually Kenyans. Eventually,

7,000 of these residents were returned to Kenya once finger-printing was introduced. Although the camp was wire-fenced, those living just outside the periphery often had some benefits from the aid which was being provided for those inside.

Fifty-one per cent of those in the camp were female, and of those 58 per cent were under 18. At the time I was there it was not a safe place to be. I had to walk through armed guards to go in and out of the camp, but there was little safeguarding, and men would come into the camp and rape women and girls there. FGM was also practised and we had people queuing for help with the results of what had happened to them. Some were unable to consummate their marriage, or if they could, it was only with great pain.

The practice of FGM was so widely accepted that of the quarter of a million people there, only sixty, from all walks of life, across the ages, and of both genders, were prepared to stand up for change and end the appalling suffering which results.

I know that if something this deeply rooted needs to change, it involves changing a whole community. So I developed a simple model: I teach you, you teach two others, who teach two more . . . changing a culture, though, can be extraordinarily difficult. One family I met demonstrated this in the most tragic way. They were a family with two parents and girls aged 6 and 8. The parents refused to subject their children to FGM. As a result, the father of the family was excluded from working at the market and the mother could not get water from the well. One of the girls was stoned and as a result lost the sight in one eye.

I now educate and campaign for the end to all gender-based violence, but particularly FGM, and I want to spend the rest of my life seeking to make a difference.

I'm often asked whether I know what happened to that little girl who had suffered so much in ways we can barely imagine.

Sadly, the answer is no. Those were different times with no mobile phones or other means of easy communication. This I do know, though. Like Naaman's servant girl all those years ago, one young refugee girl in the most extreme of situations had more effect than she could ever have imagined.

2

Living with Depression

> *Mental pain is less dramatic than physical pain,*
> *but it is more common and also more hard to*
> *bear. The frequent attempt to conceal mental*
> *pain increases the burden: it is easier to say 'My*
> *tooth is aching' than to say 'My heart is broken'.*
>
> *CS Lewis*[1]

Hearing a Voice from the Past

It is very hard to pinpoint when the darkness actually fell.
Somehow it has crept up on me like an animal stalking its
prey. I've long followed God, tried to walk well. Yet life has
been tough. You are told, aren't you, that if you follow God
everything will go well, that if it doesn't then you have sin
somewhere. I'm just not sure I can believe it is that simple any
more. Maybe it never was.

Yes, I can look back and see when God has helped me. All
life is from him, so mine is too. He must have been there from
before I was born. As I track back I am trying to be thankful,
to see how, when everything else has been shifting sands, he has
been the one solid thing in my life. My friendship with him has

been like a safe, warm cave, protection against the cold winter nights and marauding beasts. But now I feel as though I have been left in the wilderness, exposed and vulnerable to every attack, the ferocity of the elements. When is God coming to my rescue?

I am confused and in darkness. I feel as though God has abandoned me, left me surrounded by critics who want to see me fail. Everywhere I go I feel as though I am being stared at, mocked. I imagine them planning how to bring me down. I just want to be left alone. I feel as though my life is slipping away, my energy being sapped by the effort of simply keeping going. Is God going to forsake me after all? What if I have come this far only for it all to slip away? I feel as though I have fallen into a chasm, swallowed up by the earth. I am afraid. I keep rehearsing all the difficult things that have happened to me, going over and over them, worrying at them like a tongue round a loose tooth. But then I have to tell myself that God can't leave me like this.

It's torture, this swinging out of control between hope in God and despair. I'm exhausted, unsure where reality lies.

Perhaps worship holds a hope for me. I have to hold on to that: that one day I will sing again with joy, even though at the moment I can see only a bleak, grey landscape. I know that in the past I have sensed God in worship, but at the moment any attempt to sing feels like a mouthful of dust. Can I sing out truths about God, even ones I am not sure of, until they become real to me again?

I'm telling myself that if I keep praising God, it will all come right. That everything stacked against me, inside and out, will somehow get dealt with. That God will come good. That he is faithful, whatever I feel.

And perhaps, in time, I may again sense his presence as I once did.

***

The Bible records the words of this unknown Psalm writer in this way, in Psalm 71:

In you, LORD, I have taken refuge;
let me never be put to shame.
² In your righteousness, rescue me and deliver me;
turn your ear to me and save me.
³ Be my rock of refuge,
to which I can always go:
give the command to save me,
for you are my rock and my fortress.
⁴ Deliver me, my God, from the hand of the wicked,
from the grasp of those who are evil and cruel.

⁵ For you have been my hope, Sovereign LORD,
my confidence since my youth.
⁶ From birth I have relied on you;
you brought me forth from my mother's womb.
I will ever praise you.
⁷ I have become a sign to many;
you are my strong refuge.
⁸ My mouth is filled with your praise,
declaring your splendour all day long.

⁹ Do not cast me away when I am old;
do not forsake me when my strength is gone.
¹⁰ For my enemies speak against me;
those who wait to kill me conspire together.

[11] They say, 'God has forsaken him;
pursue him and seize him,
for no one will rescue him.'
[12] Do not be far from me, my God;
come quickly, God, to help me.
[13] May my accusers perish in shame;
may those who want to harm me
be covered with scorn and disgrace.

[14] As for me, I will always have hope;
I will praise you more and more.

[15] My mouth will tell of your righteous deeds,
of your saving acts all day long –
though I know not how to relate them all.
[16] I will come and proclaim your mighty acts, Sovereign Lord;
I will proclaim your righteous deeds, yours alone.
[17] Since my youth, God, you have taught me,
and to this day I declare your marvellous deeds.
[18] Even when I am old and grey,
do not forsake me, my God,
till I declare your power to the next generation,
your mighty acts to all who are to come.

[19] Your righteousness, God, reaches to the heavens,
you who have done great things.
Who is like you, God?
[20] Though you have made me see troubles,
many and bitter,
you will restore my life again;
from the depths of the earth
you will again bring me up.

²¹ You will increase my honour
and comfort me once more.

²² I will praise you with the harp
for your faithfulness, my God;
I will sing praise to you with the lyre,
Holy One of Israel.
²³ My lips will shout for joy
when I sing praise to you –
I whom you have delivered.
²⁴ My tongue will tell of your righteous acts
all day long,
for those who wanted to harm me
have been put to shame and confusion.

Although it is often assumed that David, the Old Testament king, wrote all the psalms, in fact they are attributed to a variety of authors. About half are designated David's, but other names include the family of Asaph, the sons of Korah (another family), and individuals named Heman, Jeduthun, Solomon, Moses and Ethan. Many commentators believe some of these names may have been added later, along with specific life circumstances where they appear at the head of the psalm.

What is clear is that the psalms of every kind were used in the worship life of the people of Israel. Even though there were community laments,[2] it seems to have been deemed important that laments which were individual were also included. We can only assume that this was because it was thought that the various psalms, though specific to that person's circumstances, could speak to any person who found echoes there from their own experience. Their inclusion validates the normality of such experiences in the spiritual life of believers.

There are a number of psalms which don't have a name attributed to them, sometimes referred to as the 'orphan psalms'. Psalm 71 is one of these and is one of the individual psalms of lament.[3] It is a psalm which drifts from one type of writing to another within its twenty-four verses, incorporating prayers for deliverance, lament for the writer's difficulties, and expressions of trust and hope for the future. In this way it reflects the experience of many people of faith as they struggle to hold on to God and to hope in difficult circumstances or in the grip of depression.

We don't know the exact circumstances of the psalm, but we can infer some things. There is clearly something from which the author longs to be delivered, which seems to involve others. This might be because they are directly oppressing him, or because either they are actually attributing his difficulties to sin, or he fears they are. This is in line with the thinking at that time[4] and is implied by verses 10, 11 and 13. Certainly he has been unjustly accused in some way, and also feels a sense of shame. He may have been older, or looking ahead to old age (v. 18): certainly he is looking back on his life and, while he can see God's faithfulness, he also accuses God of making him see 'many and bitter' troubles. He obviously feels in the present that God is far away from him, in contrast with the past. Yet he looks ahead – 'I will . . .' – with a sense of hope that his joy will return. In this way it is a contrast to (the named) Psalm 88, where the sense of hope is missing, closing with the desolate words: 'You have taken from me friend and neighbour – darkness is my closest friend.'[5]

In my opinion, there is a great need for lament to be included in our worship. People come on Sunday in very different places practically and emotionally, and at times attend even though in great personal pain, such as after a bereavement,

with life-limiting illness, or in the middle of relationship difficulties. In addition, a church can be traumatised by a series of
pastoral events – one church in which I served experienced the
death of a baby, the sudden death of a church worker and the
suicide of another church member in short succession, leaving
the church community reeling. At such times, to simply carry
on with triumphal, upbeat worship, declaring God is good,
whilst true, may be too simplistic to serve a congregation well.
An honest public recognition that life can be very tough, times
of silence, and the use of the psalms as a basis for prayer can be
helpful and a step towards healing.

***

Depression, sadly, is not confined to the biblical record, but all
too common in modern life. Here is one voice among so many:

Hearing a Voice from the Present

I cannot see, even looking back, a clear moment when the depression started. Rather, like twilight on a cloudy day, it crept
slowly (and ultimately insidiously) across my inner horizon,
so that I only realised it had done so when I could not see any
more. Looking back, I can trace contributing factors: several
life changes including a new and demanding job, the death of
my father who was my second parent to die and so the end of
the generation above me, and a number of major unresolved issues from a complex childhood. Perhaps I should have realised
that you can't outrun these things. Denial only lasts so long.

What I do know is that there came a point in my running
when I hit a brick wall. I just didn't want to do anything. It was

as though, like some machine in a children's story, something had sucked the colour out of everything, leaving it all an insipid grey. But no superhero came to return the colour, and as days dragged into weeks I knew that something was badly wrong.

It is difficult to describe to someone who has never been depressed what it feels like. It is as though you are walking through your life with leaden feet. I had no energy for anything, yet kept going somehow. My previous alert mind and clear thinking deserted me, but my feelings were either numbed or overwhelming with no safe middle ground. At times tears came readily and unwanted; at other times I felt nothing at all. I believed I was utterly worthless: more than that I feared I was a scourge, some cosmic accident who would damage others I came into contact with. I longed for human comfort, yet didn't want to see anyone. It was as though I had fallen into a deep pit, but with no footholds to help me crawl back out and no hope of rescue. The best I could hope for was a few hours oblivion at night, but even then I was often disturbed by nightmares. If briefly reprieved by sleep, I would wake with dread at the prospect of another day. In time I began to drink excessive alcohol to try to dull the pain, but even this liquid anaesthetic offered no real relief. I felt utterly alone, with no light on the horizon.

I dragged myself into work, painting on a smile. Perhaps a previous career in acting helped. At times, crossing the road to get there, I longed to simply throw myself under any oncoming bus. On more than one occasion I lined up tablets ready for the ultimate escape. Somehow I never did, held back a little by the effect on those around me: unwell as I was, I harboured the desire to protect others in any way possible from myself.

I had a Christian faith, but in that long time of darkness it felt at times more a hindrance than a help. Initially I confided in a house group leader at the church, a large church with lively worship. She listened, and said she would pray and come back to me with anything she thought God was saying. That was the last time she spoke to me. I presumed God didn't have anything to say. The internet, and some Christian books, offered solutions which I could not reach and which only added to my self-loathing, some implying I lacked faith, or even had some secret sin. Yet I longed to rediscover God, to find him amid my growing despair.

Even more painful was the unexpected anger I felt in worship. I found myself wanting to throw things at well-meaning preachers who seemed to offer a simplistic, rose-tinted view of life and more than once picked up a hymn-book to arm myself. I was longing for God to show me that he was there, and loved me. I attended meetings where people would single others out for a word of encouragement or prophecy, but they never came for me. I went to places where people were 'slain in the Spirit' and claimed it was a healing experience, but I always remained upright, literally the last person standing on what looked like a battlefield, yet I felt I was the one dying inside. I misremembered the story of the match girl;[6] in my internal version there was no hope or solace, but I was continually looking in at others enjoying the feast (of worship and God's presence) while I froze to death, inside the church building but excluded from any warmth of blessing. I kept singing the songs, but they had no meaning for me, not helped perhaps by the celebratory style of worship and the unquestioning certainty of the theology offered in both songs and preaching.

The turning point came with a series of events in which, now, looking back, I see the grace of God. Two people came into my darkest place who were determined to hang on in there with me, walk with me, for as long as it took: one a counsellor and one a friend. They hung on to hope for me when I had none for myself. They listened, with no shred of judgement and no facile answers. Their sheer dogged determination not to quit spoke without words of a God who was there, Immanuel in the inner mess that I thought no one could bear to see. They were God with skin on, companions in the darkness.

Another part of my recovery was writing. I wrote from the depths of despair, but trying to find a language for my desolation took a little of the pain away. Two things helped me to persist with trying to find words and believe that God might be in the attempt. One was realising that in the Psalms, the worship book of the Jewish people, the writers gave voice to their despair. I particularly found help in the psalms of lament, as the authors wrestled with their circumstances and despair alongside a desire to hold on to God and hope that again they might worship him. Psalm 88 does not resolve, as most of the psalms of lament do, to a place of worship or trust, but ends in verse 18 with words I understood only too well: 'darkness is my closest friend'.

Sometimes what I wrote was very bleak: yet it was beginning to edge towards an understanding that God was not as remote as I feared, and particularly that Jesus, on the cross, experienced our darkness in every sense.

Crucifixion

There are
No words.
Only screaming
Silent agony
Black despair
No future
Only death
Utterly alone
And lost

In all
The universe.
No light
No sign
Of grace
No place
To hide
No shelter
No arms
To hold.
Only instead
Limitless grief
Overwhelming rage
Paralysing terror
Helplessly trapped
An end
To good
No end
To pain
No rescue
No one
To care
To see
To understand
Reach out
Or touch
And find.
Hope lost
An eternity
Of isolation.
Only silence
And darkness.

This, then,
Is hell.

As hope stirred a little, it showed itself in glimmers of light in
my poetry. This one was entitled 'Courage':

Courage –
Like love –
Comes in
Many kinds.

Maybe what
Is sometimes needed
Is not the obvious forms
Of battle heroism
Or foolish assumption
Of untouchable invincibility.

But instead
Recognising our vulnerability
We can still
Lift our eyes
From the dust
And sing
In the darkness
As somehow
We find the strength
To choose the path
We have not chosen
And walk it
In the hope
Of his grace.

It was a long road to crawl to recovery: years, not months. Just as it was difficult to see the fog descend, so there was no one moment when it lifted, more a slow dissolving as the sun rose over my shattered life. I was able to occasionally genuinely smile, and then laugh. The inner wounds, whilst not fully healed, began to have more tolerable levels of pain, and I could see their size, shape and origin. I slowly rediscovered joy in the ordinary.

I would love to end here saying that the darkness never returns, but it wouldn't be true. It does, sometimes, though it has never revisited with the same ferocity or for as long. I have learned better strategies than a futile denial, including heading back to the Psalms. But I certainly don't have it sorted. I still wrestle at times with my view of myself and need wise friends to gently hold up a truer mirror. What I do know, though, is that like the Psalms there is a place for lament in my worship; for pouring everything out to God, taking it to him with all its rawness, anger and vulnerability. It is a sign of intimacy and not distance: that he alone can see that part of me and understand, not condemn.

And perhaps, in time, he may yet give me 'the treasures of darkness'.[7]

3

Searching for Meaning

Utterly meaningless! Everything is meaningless.[1]
Solomon

Hearing a Voice from the Past

I've always been searching – searching for the truth, about the world, about myself, about God. And that searching has taken me to the most unlikely of places . . .

I've always asked questions too – I suppose it must be in my nature, though my teachers have been the natural world, philosophy and the religious writings of various faiths. Everything I have learned has led me to see a complex world and to have the desperate need to find purpose in it all.

Not that I could have complained. I was well off, with plenty to live on, as well as having the prestige of my occupation and the love of my family. Life was good. Yet still I was left wondering – is there more?

So night after night I studied the stars, searching for meaning as they cast their iridescent lights through the sapphire sky. Across my land there was a mysterious but significant sense of growing anticipation, as if the very air was alive with expectancy. Somehow I felt as though creation had to mark this, because the impact would be not just on us, or humanity, but on the whole created order.

Nor was I the only one. My companions, other teachers and students, sensed it too. Yet weeks, then months passed, and still nothing. I began to doubt. Perhaps I had been mistaken. Perhaps this was all there is, and I must settle for my studies and the dreary but settled routine of my everyday life.

Until that night. At first I thought I was mistaken; that despondency and desire had blended to give my wishful thoughts substance. I stopped, shook myself, and looked again. No, it was definitely there.

I ran through the night to my friend's house. I needed confirmation that what I was seeing was real. But as I approached his house he burst through the front opening, apparently on his way to find me. We went inside and sat for hours talking about what it might mean, and looking, again and again. We were joined by others from our group who had seen it too. The air was thick with our excitement. None of us slept much that night, and the next day we were weary, yet restless and edgy, unsure what to do next. For several days we talked in circles, endlessly rehearsing possibilities, weighing practicalities, fear alternating with exhilaration.

In the end, I forced a decision, telling the others that I was going to go, either alone, or with them. My need to know, to find out, finally outweighed every caution. Some could not join me, of course, but there were enough of us willing to go to make this quest as safe as it could be, taking the gamble. My family were not pleased – their reactions varying from irritation at my desertion to bluntly questioning my sanity. But, in the end, they could see there was no stopping me and so reluctantly gave me their support for what they dubbed my 'fool's errand'. I set about gathering provisions.

And so the night came, the start of my adventure into the unknown. Amid the inky darkness I said goodbye to my tearful family, resolute yet troubled that I was unable to give them any assurance when, or even if, I would return. We were following, yet not knowing exactly where.

Travel by camel is arduous even for the shortest time, and there were points when I thought my body might give out altogether. I longed for the comforts of home, for clean sheets and welcoming smiles. At different times each of us fell ill. At one point, as one of my companions wrestled with a virulent fever that would not abate whatever we did, I feared we might not all reach our destination. But we were unwavering in our search and determined not to be turned back.

All our studies, and the inexplicable rumours of our era had suggested the place to head for was Judea. For some reason this small area of our world had always had more significance than its size warranted. By this time we had no visual clue to follow, and so we used our logic and headed to the king's palace. Surely that was the place where a king would be born.

It was not that Herod was discourteous. Far from it. But something in my spirit made me profoundly uneasy. It was as if there was a malaise there, a deep sickness, which I could not describe but which pervaded the very atmosphere and choked my soul. He brought scores of experts, parading them before us like his personal trophies, as if to show us how powerful he was, never seeming to realise, or to care, that we were people of rank in our own culture.

They were useful, though. They were adamant that their expected Messiah would be born not in Jerusalem but in Bethlehem. I secretly hoped the air would be sweeter there than this stifling air of greed and – it seemed to me – suppressed violence.

Herod seemed content for us to go alone, but just before we left he called us into his throne room. Sitting aloft, in what seemed to me an unabashed power-play, he said in a most obsequious manner, 'Just one more question . . . when exactly did you see this sign?' We told him – we had nothing to hide. His final words to us were: '*Go and search carefully for the child. As soon as you find him, report to me, so that I too may go and worship him.*'[2]

So again we set off. We left at sunset, still a little unsure. But then – and I can't tell you the sheer unadulterated joy and delight, as if our hearts would burst! – there it was again. We followed carefully, a much quicker journey than the one to Judea, and our excitement rose as we reached what we thought was our journey's end.

The house was unassuming, and for a moment we were dubious. But we were let in at once, strangers in an unfamiliar land greeted as though it were the most natural thing in the world, as though we were already family.

And then we saw him. An ordinary boy, on his mother's knee. A sight we had all seen a hundred times. Such weakness, such vulnerability. Yet all of us, without a moment's hesitation, prostrated ourselves before him without a single thought for our status or our dignity. I knew that my search was finally over. Here in this child were wrapped up all my longings, all the failures of the past which were somehow no longer significant, and a whole new future which was still to open up. We gave him the gifts we had brought, but without speaking a word he offered us so much more.

The disquiet we had felt at the palace spilled out that night in dreams and we decided to take another route back. It might have seemed like the end of the adventure. But each of us knew, without ever having to voice it, that it was just the beginning.

***

Matthew 2:1–12 expresses it this way:

After Jesus was born in Bethlehem in Judea, during the time of King Herod, Magi from the east came to Jerusalem ² and asked, 'Where is the one who has been born king of the Jews? We saw his star when it rose and have come to worship him.'

³ When King Herod heard this he was disturbed, and all Jerusalem with him. ⁴ When he had called together all the people's chief priests and teachers of the law, he asked them where the Messiah was to be born. ⁵ 'In Bethlehem in Judea,' they replied, 'for this is what the prophet has written:

⁶ '"But you, Bethlehem, in the land of Judah,
are by no means least among the rulers of Judah;
for out of you will come a ruler
who will shepherd my people Israel."'

⁷ Then Herod called the Magi secretly and found out from them the exact time the star had appeared. ⁸ He sent them to Bethlehem and said, 'Go and search carefully for the child. As soon as you find him, report to me, so that I too may go and worship him.'

⁹ After they had heard the king, they went on their way, and the star they had seen when it rose went ahead of them until it stopped over the place where the child was. ¹⁰ When they saw the star, they were overjoyed. ¹¹ On coming to the house, they saw the child with his mother Mary, and they bowed down and worshipped him. Then they opened their treasures and presented him with gifts of gold, frankincense and myrrh. ¹² And having been warned in a dream not to go back to Herod, they returned to their country by another route.

It's the stuff of every children's nativity play, isn't it? Just three kings, dressed in gaudy colours (in contrast to large numbers of

shepherds with tea towel head coverings) carefully (or not so carefully) carrying one gift each, of gold, frankincense and myrrh,
and coming to kneel at the crib with baby Jesus. They may
well even be named in the script as Caspar, Balthasar, and
Melchior or similar variations, or the carol 'We Three Kings'
sung. A lesser known carol, called 'When Wise Men Came
Seeking', includes these words:

> They found in a stable the Savior of men,
> A manger His cradle, so poor was He then.[3]

This popularist version of the story has led people to enjoy it at
Christmas but dismiss it as a lovely story yet with no factual basis.
However, careful reading of the account in Matthew tells a very dif-
ferent story in which these legendary elements are actually missing.

Matthew begins his account of the visit of the wise men without any description of Jesus' birth but simply with a placing of
it in time and geography – in the time of King Herod, so prior
to 4BC[4] when Herod died, and in Bethlehem – he specifies the
Judean Bethlehem as there was one in Galilee, near Nazareth.
The Bethlehem of Jesus' birth was a small town about six miles
south of the capital Jerusalem, with a long history dating back
to the Jewish patriarch Jacob burying his beloved Rachel.[5]

Matthew then reports that Magi (not kings,[6] and no numbers attached – that has come from the three gifts which, of
course, does not automatically mean three individuals) come
to Jerusalem *'from the east'*. Who are these Magi? Most commentators assume, with good reason, that they were astrologers
from either Persia or Babylon, today's equivalent being Iran
and Iraq. They would have been scientists rather than for-
tune tellers, people who seriously studied the stars in line with
the ancient belief that any major events, including the birth

of somebody significant, would be shown in the skies.[7] This demonstrates a conviction, which is not at all unbiblical, that we are part of a wider cosmos with which we are deeply connected.[8] Theirs was also a culture for whom artificial light and the pollution of streetlights was unknown. They were much more aware of, and in touch with, the night sky than we are in the West today.

There is another interesting link here. Some centuries before this, the term 'Magi' had been used of a priestly caste of Medes, a group living in what is now north-western Iran. They were known for natural science, and wisdom in various areas including interpreting dreams. Those familiar with the Bible (or even biblical children's stories) may immediately link interpreting dreams with the Old Testament character Daniel. In the account of Daniel's exile in nearby Babylon, *'magoi'* are mentioned.[9] The book of Daniel contains a number of prophecies about the Messiah to come. It is possible that the stories of a coming leader for all nations were passed down from Daniel's time in these communities of interested scientist/astrologers as well as being kept alive in the large colony of Jews who stayed in Babylon when most of their countrymen returned from the exile.

Matthew does not give too much detail as to what exactly the Magi saw, only that they saw it 'when it rose'. There has been much resulting speculation[10] but the reality is that we can't know. They clearly saw some form of astrological phenomena, and knew (either for the reasons cited above or from studies of Jewish writing) of the expectation of the birth of a new leader bringing a new era of peace. There have been suggestions that these expectations of a new world leader emerging may have even been widespread at the time – based on some of the Roman historians such as Suetonius and Tacitus.[11]

Whatever they saw, it was in nature, and the relationship of Christians with creation has varied enormously. Sometimes there has been an element of caution – for example, because of concerns that if we become too connected with nature we will espouse pantheism.[12] However, there is a vast difference between worshipping the God who created nature and worshipping nature itself. This ambivalent relationship with the created world has at times been fuelled by an attitude which says that if God is going to fashion a new heaven and earth[13] then there is no need to care for the existing one. However, the Bible makes clear in many places that nature expresses who God is, and so if *'The heavens declare the glory of God; the skies proclaim the work of his hands'*[14] it should not surprise us at all that at the incarnation of God's Son, through whom everything was made,[15] God should speak to spiritual searchers through his creation. Many people have found that this experience of God through nature is still the case.[16]

As a result of what they saw, they decided to make the long journey to seek out the new king – they must have been wealthy to have the means to do so. Understandably, they first come to Jerusalem, the capital where they would have expected any new king to be born. Herod the Great,[17] however, is a king like no other. As we will be reminded again in chapter 6, Herod, a schemer who had taken advantage of Roman political unrest to claw his way to the top, has become a ruthless and insecure tyrant. He was also a gifted individual with some significant achievements. He strengthened Israel's position in the ancient world by increasing its commerce and turning it into a trading hub for Arabia and the East. His massive building programme included theatres, amphitheatres, a port, markets, temples, housing, palaces, walls around Jerusalem and aqueducts. He even had moments of compassion in times of famine.

However, he was a brutal man who killed several of his family, including two of his sons. The Roman Emperor, Augustus, famously said it was safer to be Herod's pig than his son.[18] This murderous streak didn't end with his death either. Just before he died, he ordered some of Jerusalem's most distinguished citizens to be arrested on trumped-up charges and sentenced to death. Their execution was to take place the minute he died. Herod knew no one would mourn his passing, but wanted to make sure that people grieved the day he died.[19]

By the time the Magi encounter him, he is an increasingly unwell man whose paranoia has grown. It is to his palace that the Magi arrive, and their message is political dynamite. If a new king has been born, Herod is not the true king. When he is troubled, fearing a threat to his throne, the whole city is caught up in his unrest as rumours of these foreign visitors circulate. Although the ordinary people might not be concerned about the birth of a potential new king, indeed they might welcome it, with Herod's track record they would certainly have been afraid of his anger.

Important as it is, the natural world alone is not enough to give these seekers the answers they require. A clearer answer comes as they study the Scriptures. We can see how seriously Herod takes this as he has called the entire Sanhedrin together, both the religious aristocracy and the theological scholars. Not being a pure-bred Jew, any threat from the line of David was very real. Herod's advisers point to the prophecy of Micah 5:2,4 and so to the significance of Bethlehem, the home town of King David,[20] from whom the Messiah is expected to descend.

Before the Magi leave, Herod calls them to a secret meeting to ascertain when they first saw the star, presumably to work out when this child was born. Given his blatant lie about wanting to worship him, and the secrecy of the meeting, sadly

we need to assume that he has already decided to liquidate this
threat to his throne by assassinating the child, which he later
attempts to do by a wider massacre when the Magi do not
return.[21] Clearly he is confident that he has deceived them as
he sends no escort with them, although certainly an accompa-
nying group of soldiers may well have jeopardised the search.

Matthew's account says the star stopped over the place where
Jesus was and that their response in seeing it is an overwhelming joy. The English does not do justice to the exuberant original. Stars do not usually stop over houses and in fact the text
does not specify that, simply saying '*the place*'. It is perhaps a
way of simply and poetically saying they were led there by what
they saw. Travelling at night was not unusual. A star was used
in connection with prophecies about the Messiah: 'A *star will
come out of Jacob; a sceptre will rise out of Israel.*'[22] Whatever
exactly they saw originally, it started them on the journey to
Jerusalem, and whatever they see at this point (clearly after a
gap, hence their delight to see it), it reassures them that they
are going in the right direction. It is reminiscent of the pillar
of cloud by day and of fire by night which guides the people
of Israel in the wilderness, a tangible sign of God's presence,
found in the book of Exodus.

So they travel on, and find their way to where Jesus is living.
Matthew specifies that the family are now in a house. Clearly
Jesus is not newborn, which makes sense if the Magi began
their long journey when he was. As Herod later had boys under
3 killed, a year or so may well have passed, giving the family
time to make the move to a house.

Having reached the end of their quest they find a vulnerable child, a radically different kind of king, in stark contrast
to Herod who wields a very different type of power. Seeing
the child, they literally fall down and worship him, men of

great stature and dignity prostrating themselves, unlike the indifferent religious elite and the hostile Herod. They present him the gifts, gold, frankincense and myrrh: giving gifts in those cultures indicated both submission and allegiance to a superior. These particular gifts are often seen as symbolic of Jesus' role and nature, gold for kingship, incense (which was used in Temple sacrifices) for worship of his deity and myrrh (used for embalming) representing his suffering and death. It is hard to know if that was the intention either of the Magi or of Matthew in recording it. They could simply have been very costly gifts, appropriate for bringing to a king. However, whatever the original significance, looking back we can see what appropriate gifts they were as Jesus' life and ministry unfolded.

Their extraordinary journey has resulted in an encounter with Jesus, and their presence at this early point of his life looks ahead to the fact that he is a king for all people, not just for Jews. Together with the earlier visit of the shepherds,[23] also interestingly unnamed, they remind us that Jesus is born for those of no status and those who are respected, for those with little education and those with a great deal. He really is born for *all* people.

They are warned not to return to Herod as he requested, an action which saves the life of the young Jesus. They go home by another route and pass into the pages of history, the rest of their story known only to God.

***

It's easy to assume that the search for God is only that initial search to find faith. But that search goes on, especially when life takes us down a route we have not chosen . . .

Hearing a Voice from the Present

I guess my road of spiritual searching will, in many ways, last a lifetime. I have always believed that there was a God, although I have doubted his existence deeply a number of times in my life. The more I journey into a thumbnail of understanding who God is, the more I realise how little I know! Which doesn't always go down well in this world we live in, a world which so often requires absolutes, facts and certainties. If that is what you are seeking from reading this tale, then sadly I will disappoint.

I cannot give facts, absolutes and certainty. What I have done is stare down the monster that robs faith and come out stronger and deeper. Here is one of those times.

In my early twenties, one of my oldest friends was diagnosed with a brain tumour. Do you know what that does to a person? I am sure you do; many of us walk the cancer path with someone, or if not with cancer, then with something else. He was an extraordinary person, and amazingly, watching from the outside, I saw his character deepen and flourish through this traumatic time. His faith grew and he became 'even more' of who he was through the enduring illness. His love for his family grew and he was so selfless. His journey with cancer was full of remission and return. I had been a strong Christian for a few years, gone to Bible college, worked with a church, seeking out how to serve God as best I could. However, praying for healing wasn't my thing. I didn't really do it easily, mainly because I didn't like facing disappointment. I remember going to a conference, and during one of the talks I was convinced that I must pray for my friend to be 'healed'. As an activist character this meant offering to pray with him and a couple of others once a week – if they were interested. They were. We prayed. God did meet us in those times. After eight weeks, he died.

How do you come back from that?

Looking into the eyes of death is so very tiring. The power-lessness, the helplessness of knowing that nothing can repair it, because there is no restoration, there is only learning some-thing new, and who wants to do that when it is the person that has gone who we just want back?

And God? God. Who was he? Where was he? How well did I know him, after all? I had believed without doubt that I should pray for my friend's healing. And my understanding of that meant, if God was involved and he had asked me to pray, then he would 'pitch up' to honour his end of the deal, which would surely mean physical healing. Wouldn't he? Apparently not. Not in this case.

It is ironic that Jesus says '*Why are you afraid?*' when the disciples are in the middle of a storm on a small fishing boat, after he has slept through most of it.[24] Fear is a big part of learning something new, and there was nothing bigger than feeling like everything that I had built life on was rocking, un-steady and unsure. It was in this state that I moved to London; a market-town girl who wasn't very brave generally, moved to the big city to work with young people who found themselves without a home. The search for meaning through the grief I was experiencing was immense. I was beset by fluctuating emotions and a constant need for acceptance. Discovering that God might accept me in that place, in any place I might find myself, was a long way off, and at that point I believed in a God who loved me when I did things for him, rather than a God who loved me unconditionally. But this was also the God with whom I was very, very angry.

I started to look for a church, and after a very long month found one, and in attending discovered I couldn't cope with it. I couldn't handle singing words I didn't mean, couldn't cope with hearing sermons that made me want to lash out. I felt isolated, remote from smiley faces telling me that this God guy in Jesus form was interested in where I was at. I had so many questions. 'If he'd been so interested, why did my friend die? Why are his parents having to deal with the deep pain? Why had I felt so sure I should pray for his healing?'

This went on for about three months, and I made some very poor choices during that time. Choices out of a need to be accepted, safe and loved in my new stage of life. Fortunately, God did have it in hand and helped me heal.

I remember very clearly being in the kitchen at the hostel where I worked and my co-worker saying, 'You need to go and have a chat with our colleague.'

'I don't need anyone,' I raged. I was determined I could cope with all of this by myself. At that moment, the person she had named walked through the door, with a resident. I found words coming out of my mouth that my heart and brain did not control, which were: 'Can I come and chat to you?'

'Yes,' she said, 'tonight at 7?'

'OK,' I said.

Truly that was out of my control. I had been so adamant that I was not going to seek help, but help was immediately available the moment I requested it. It had been fear, fear of the anger, of rejection if my real self was seen, that was holding me back from asking.

Sharing my pain was such a cathartic experience, and admitting anger that I was unaware of was deeply healing. As my colleague prayed with me, she shared a picture of a tiny sailing boat on calm waters. She wondered if God wanted me to be the sailing boat and allow him to be the wind that set the course. In her waiting and praying, and my allowing the space to envelop my hurt, it began to diminish a little.

My pain didn't go, but my anger did. The sadness of the loss of my friend and the ache for the suffering of his family and friends will never leave me. However, it has deepened my faith and revealed another layer of the many pictures of who God is. As I search deeper for who he is throughout my life, I am learning more than anything that however difficult the road gets for me, God, through Jesus, proves trustworthy every time.

4

The Impact of Forgiveness

Be even-tempered, content with second place,
quick to forgive an offense. Forgive as quickly
and completely as the Master forgave you.[1]

Paul

Hearing a Voice from the Past

Some things eat away at you, like vultures on a decaying carcass.
You shoo them away for a moment, but they come back, flying
in and taking up residence again. You are never rid of them.

That was how it felt for me. I never understood how things
came about: did my own guilt cause the illness, was it a punish-
ment from God, or did the remorse and sickness just co-exist,
uneasy bedfellows in my soul? I didn't know. Plenty of people
were happy to give me their opinion, of course. Especially religious people, who seem to carry their sense of being right like
a trophy. But I was never sure.

What I did know was that I could never shake off the things
in my life that I had done wrong. Some small things, which
perhaps others would have shrugged off, but I never could.
And some immense things, the memory of which frequently

woke me, my heart pounding as if my chest would be crushed with the burden of it all. I replayed every failure, the ending never changing. I felt caught in a trap of my own making.

Then there were the things other people had done to me. I stored them up too, a putrefying hoard which I knew I should not keep but somehow could not part with. I could not release my pain, and as time went by I nursed my resentments like sick children who needed care. I knew this was not what I wanted, but I couldn't find any way out of the prison I was in.

Daily life continued until one day I woke with a sense of unease that something was not right in my body. I carried on, but as the days went by the weakness grew until I could not walk. I was terrified. We tried doctors but nothing worked, and in the end they just shook their heads and walked away. Unlike me. I couldn't walk anywhere. I was terrified. Who was going to provide for my wife and children? Was this how I was going to die?

I hated feeling helpless and dependent. It was agony watching those busy around me, my wife exhausting herself in doing all my tasks as well as her own. They would prop me up so that I could watch the children play in the street, but when they tripped and cried I could not scoop them up in my arms to comfort them. My friends were faithful in visiting, but their visits were bittersweet – I could see the pity for me in their eyes and I felt less of a man somehow. The days and nights, then the weeks and months, stretched drearily into each other until all hope drained away.

You can't keep anything quiet in a fishing village like Capernaum. So when Simon, Andrew, James and John left their fishing business for others to run and started following a young rabbi called Jesus, we all heard about it – and we were astonished. After all, the other rabbis had already chosen the bright among us, those with religious promise – who was this one who chose ordinary fishermen and, as we later heard, even the local tax collector, Levi, to disciple?

Then came the stories of the miracles. The accounts were shocking – an exorcism in the synagogue, Simon's mother-in-law being healed, and many in the crowds who flocked to hear him finding freedom. Apparently, his teaching was also like no one else's – not just quoting others, but speaking for himself. Then came the most scandalous story of all – a leper, one of our town, came to the priest and was declared clean, saying Jesus had healed him. People were cautious of the (ex-) leper at first, but soon it was obvious he was well and he would tell anyone who would listen that Jesus had restored him – by touching him. *Touching* him? Who was this man, to touch and heal even a leper?

I thought about him sometimes, wondered if he could help me. He was based here, but came and went, and then one day we heard he was back again. I had nothing to lose, so got my wife to ask four of our friends to take me to see him. I hated going out by then, seeing the stares as I was carried past, but I was desperate. My friends were only too willing, saying they knew Jesus could help and were going to offer anyway.

When we arrived at the house, disappointment and despair washed over me again. I should have thought about the crowds. There was no way we could get anywhere near him: the room was full, with people spilling out into the street. I steeled myself for the journey home, but my friends were not going to be so easily deterred. I heard them whispering, but could not hear what they were saying. Then, to my bewilderment, two of them climbed the stairs to the roof. I had no idea what they were doing, and then with horror I realised they were cracking the clay and moving aside the branches to make a hole in the roof. I was appalled. These were people I knew, dirt showering on their heads! What would Jesus say – would he be angry at having his teaching interrupted? However, nothing was going to stop them, and the next thing I knew I was being carried up the steps and then lowered down through the hole they had made. They had obviously thought ahead, unlike me, and brought ropes to get me in. I closed my eyes, so as not to see either my precarious journey down to the floor or the reaction of the bystanders whose prime view of Jesus was being disrupted by this unwelcome intrusion.

The pallet came to rest and I knew I was safely on the ground. Cautiously, I opened my eyes. There he was. I'm not sure what I expected, but he seemed surprisingly ordinary. He was watching my companions, hot and grimy from their exertion, looking back at him with hope and expectation. Then he looked down at me and I had to glance away. After a moment, he spoke. '*Son, your sins are forgiven.*'[2] I'd not been called someone's child in a long time, and never in a way like that. It was as though he came into the dark to call me out of a nightmare and reassure me that it was alright: no one was angry with me and I was safe.

As I looked up and finally really caught his gaze, it is hard to describe what I saw. Somewhere I could hear the gasps of the crowd at his words, but I did not register them. There was a fire in his eyes, as though the things I had done and the things which had been done to me really mattered, hurt him as they had hurt me and yes, made him angry. Yet there was a gentleness there too, a tenderness which felt deeply all the pain and struggle, a compassion which was the deepest thing of all and which ached for every regret which had paralysed my soul. My eyes filled with tears.

Just at that moment Jesus looked away at the crowd. He held the gaze of the religious leaders in particular, who were bristling with self-righteous offence. Then I heard him say, with quiet challenge, '*Why are you thinking these things? Which is easier: to say to this paralysed man, "Your sins are forgiven," or to say, "Get up, take your mat and walk"? But I want you to know that the Son of Man has authority on earth to forgive sins.'*[3]

I had hardly had time to think about the enormity of his claim when he turned back to me and again held my gaze. *'Get up, take your mat and go home.'*[4] Rise up? That would be as impossible as resurrection! I opened my mouth to say I couldn't, I was paralysed, but as I again saw the warmth which emanated from him I started to move, finding to my astonishment that my limbs did what I told them. In a rush strength returned, and I got to my feet, picked up my bed and made my way through the crowd, who parted in astonishment to let me through. I was healed. In every way.

So in that one moment my life was restored. I still keep that bed, propped up in a corner, the frayed material curled round the poles. It is a reminder to me to keep walking in the freedom that he gave me that day.

Jesus has made me new.

***

Mark 2:1–12 tells us the story:

A few days later, when Jesus again entered Capernaum, the people heard that he had come home. [2] They gathered in such large numbers that there was no room left, not even outside the door, and he preached the word to them. [3] Some men came, bringing to him a paralysed man, carried by four of them. [4] Since they could not get him to Jesus because of the crowd, they made an opening in the roof above Jesus by digging through it and then lowered the mat the man was lying on. [5] When Jesus saw their faith, he said to the paralysed man, 'Son, your sins are forgiven.'

⁶ Now some teachers of the law were sitting there, thinking to themselves, ⁷'Why does this fellow talk like that? He's blaspheming! Who can forgive sins but God alone?'

⁸ Immediately Jesus knew in his spirit that this was what they were thinking in their hearts, and he said to them, 'Why are you thinking these things? ⁹Which is easier: to say to this paralysed man, "Your sins are forgiven," or to say, "Get up, take your mat and walk"? ¹⁰ But I want you to know that the Son of Man has authority on earth to forgive sins.' So he said to the man, ¹¹'I tell you, get up, take your mat and go home.' ¹²He got up, took his mat and walked out in full view of them all. This amazed everyone and they praised God, saying, 'We have never seen anything like this!'

This vivid and shocking story takes place, Mark⁵ tells us, in Capernaum, a fishing village on the northern shore of the Sea of Galilee. At this point of Jesus' life, he has moved his base there from Nazareth (he was born in Bethlehem, spent time as a refugee in Egypt and then his parents returned to their home town of Nazareth), going from there to preach in the surrounding synagogues and villages. It is therefore possible that this was the house that Jesus himself was using.⁶ If that is the case, it was his roof which was partially ruined by the little group determined to make sure their friend got to Jesus. Most ordinary houses were simple, with a door on to the street, and would have been quickly filled with those eager to hear Jesus. Roofs were usually flat, constructed of beams with the spaces between them packed with small branches and clay or tiles. They were used in various ways so usually had a simple stairway on the outside going up to them. Certainly, when it says Jesus saw their faith (presumably faith that he could do something to help), he was referring to the persistence of these men: but also, from the willingness to be brought and the response in getting up, it may well be that the paralysed man also had at least some faith.

Remarkable as the physical healing is, the shocking element in the story and its main emphasis is Jesus declaring the man's sins forgiven. There was widespread belief at that time that sickness was caused by sin,[7] but Jesus did not teach this and on one occasion directly contradicted it,[8] so it is unclear why it was Jesus' starting point for this particular healing. Was he simply operating from a mindset that would make sense to everyone there? Was it that the man himself, accepting popular teaching, would not have believed it was possible for him to be healed until he was forgiven? Was it because Jesus saw something pressing in the man's spiritual state, or even a psychosomatic element to his paralysis?[9] Or was it a deliberate challenge to the religious leaders present, an indication of his true identity? Perhaps there were elements of some or all of these.

The teachers of the law were there – the scribes, who were mainly also Pharisees and who were experts in the details of the Jewish legal traditions. It is unclear if their presence was originally out of genuine curiosity or interest, or to check Jesus out as self-appointed guardians of orthodoxy. It was part of their duty to deal with any false prophets who could easily unhelpfully sway the people, which was actually at times a valid role in calming volatility in the turbulent atmosphere of foreign occupation. Jesus senses their inner questioning. The scribes, of course, were theologically correct, in the sense that it is only God who can forgive sins.[10] To declare someone's sins forgiven was something only priests could do and, even then, only in the name of God. The Temple was the place where sacrifices were made to enable sins to be forgiven. For a man who was not a priest and not involved in Temple worship to declare forgiveness was unthinkable.

Jesus did not dispute that only God could forgive sins. If he was saying these words as a mere human then, yes, it was blasphemy, punishable in their society by stoning.[11] Instead Jesus challenges them with the rabbinical-style question: '*Why are you thinking these things? Which is easier: to say to this paralysed man, "Your sins are forgiven," or to say, "Get up, take your mat and walk"?* Of course, to simply speak the words '*your sins are forgiven*' is easier in one sense. To declare someone's sins forgiven has no external sign and so cannot be proved one way or the other. However, to the scribes this was the more difficult thing to say, since only God could forgive sins.

So Jesus in essence says – to show I have the right to declare this man's sins forgiven, the harder thing, I will do the lesser thing and heal him. To link the declaration of forgiveness with physical healing showed that Jesus had enormous confidence in his own identity and power in the situation. One of the hallmarks of the stories told about Jesus was that he demonstrated a unique quiet authority, and we see this again here. By linking forgiveness and healing, Jesus stamps that authority on both the spiritual and the physical realm,[12] as well as setting in motion a conflict with the religious leaders which would ultimately result in his death.[13] No wonder the crowd were amazed.

Jesus refers to himself in this passage as the '*Son of Man*', a title he often used of himself[14] and which was a title used by Jews of the coming Messiah. To fully understand this title, we need to look back to Daniel 7, especially verses 13,14. Described in that passage is someone '*like a son of man*' who represents God's people. There is opposition to God and his people, but the Son of Man prevails and God gives him authority.

The area of forgiveness is a huge one and would merit a whole book to itself, and indeed there are many on the subject.[15] It was central to a great deal of Jesus' teaching, including several parables[16] and is included in the model prayer Jesus taught his disciples: '*Forgive us our sins, for we also forgive every-one who sins against us.*'[17] On the cross, Jesus demonstrated his forgiveness even of those persecuting him: '*Father, forgive them, for they do not know what they are doing.*'[18]

To forgive someone does not mean that what they did is right – quite the reverse. If it was not wrong, it would not need forgiveness. Our forgiveness of others is often a process which needs revisiting as hurts resurface – forgiveness is not about forgetting and to link the two is unhelpful. To seek to forgive also does not mean that there will not be consequences, legal or otherwise, or that any relationships between people involved can be restored. In the case of violence or abuse, it may well not be safe to do so. Forgiveness *does* mean no longer holding them to account to us or seeking any kind of vengeance, as well as working towards dealing with the anger and resentment we feel because of what they have done to us.

The forgiveness that we receive from God is very different from that which we give each other, since as people we are all flawed. The relationship with God is different, God granting us forgiveness so that we can be in friendship with him – we have wronged him but he has not wronged us. The death of Jesus reminds us that forgiveness was very costly. On the cross Jesus stretches out his arms in welcome to us, beckoning us home, at the cost of his life. All forgiveness is costly.

The giving and receiving of forgiveness is as huge an issue in the world now as it was then, impacting individuals and whole societies. To give forgiveness is sacrificial and to receive it requires honesty and humility. However, both receiving and giving forgiveness are essential to anyone who would seek to follow Jesus. It is a difficult, but essential, road to travel.

***

Hearing a Voice from the Present

I was somewhere between 7 and 8, and at a convent school. It had been a tough year – my form teacher at the school had died, and my only remaining grandmother had too. She had been my main older role model. I was an only child, and looking back I realise I was vulnerable.

At the school I attended, there was a priest who took communion for the children and carried various other responsibilities. I had been playing sport and ran inside. Coming in from a light playground to a darker interior I didn't see him and I literally ran into him. He asked me to take him to another part of the building and though I pointed it out to him, he insisted I take him there. He was a person of authority and I felt I had no choice. He abused me there and I never returned to my lesson.

I arrived home late and tearful and told my mother everything. She reported it to the school. He was sent away, but others who did not know the situation were devastated at his loss. There was even less support at that time than now and I was alone with everything I had experienced and the feelings I was left with.

The abuse I suffered affected everything about my life – and still does. There are so many terrible legacies from abuse, which differ from person to person but which, whether hidden or overt, are paralysing. Some people trust nobody, others trust unwisely in the hope of somehow putting something right. It is easy for those who have suffered abuse to feel responsible for what happened to them – sometimes abusers cause this directly by what they say or threaten, at other times it is simply the way a child seeks to make sense of the inexplicable. It affects how people see themselves and see others and the nature of their relationships for the rest of their lives. The desperation to be truly loved runs very deep and makes survivors vulnerable to exploitation. If abused people are able to have children, when their children reach the same age as significant events, this can trigger flashbacks or renewed pain. Knowing their children are receiving something they never had – safety and love – whilst healing in one way by breaking the cycle, is an ever-present painful reminder of the yawning gap within. It is easy to become hyper-sensitive, fearing that the ordinary ups and downs of relationships may signify the approach of some form of disaster. Somehow there is always a search for someone who will not let them down, take care of them safely and without exploitation. Yet this is destined for disappointment as eventually people, who are all flawed and broken, do let them down. These are just a few of the numerous ways abuse impacts people as adults.[19]

The effect on me was as great as it is for others. I developed an eating disorder and had great difficulty in forming relationships. Deep down I believed other people would always let me down, yet I over-trusted and that proved as damaging as isolation would have been. I did marry, but realised looking back that my husband had actually been grooming me from the day we met. He had picked up on my vulnerability and became abusive from the day we married: setting rules for our relationship on the wedding night which I broke at my peril.

In time my husband left – very quickly entering another relationship. I had a Christian faith, though I had converted to Judaism. I began to realise that part of my journey towards healing meant confronting the reality of the past and perhaps beginning to take steps towards forgiving those who had so damaged me.

I went to see the Mother Superior in the convent where the school was based, who was now in her eighties. By this time it was thirty-five years after the abuse, but she remembered. I found that the priest had entered a silent order and she said simply, 'He has had a lot of years to think about the error of his ways.' I got some holy water and watered a tree in his name in recognition of my journey of forgiveness.

The time came when I was due to be stationed abroad with my work to an area of some danger, and I asked to meet up with my ex-husband. When we did, he asked me why I had wanted to do so. I explained that I did not want to face death with things sitting between us. He expressed regret for what he had done. I realise that sometimes we have to offer forgiveness when the other person will not recognise that they have done anything wrong (or at times when the person has already died), but for me it helped that he was able to say that. I have laid down any expectation of marrying again, however. I know my capacity to trust someone to that degree is damaged, I suspect beyond repair. Despite everything, I have never broken my wedding vows, but the trampling over them by his abuse has made me very, very wary.

One of the often unacknowledged results of abuse is that something, obvious or apparently minor, which carries an echo of the past can reawaken the most intense pain and stress, years and even decades later. Just last summer I took a trip to Lourdes with a friend and happened on part of the journey to find myself sitting next to a priest in the same order as my abuser. All of the hurt and distress came rushing back at the visible reminder unwittingly carried by my companion. I knew my abuser had died. I discovered in conversation that he had been sent abroad in later years and I worry that he may have damaged other vulnerable children. Hearing this story caused me to break two teeth – a stress fracture – as I felt 'trapped' on the coach.

The journey towards forgiveness is a long one. Perhaps it is never complete, as new events bring back the pain. Even scars can hurt. Sometimes, sadly, communities of faith can be places where abuse occurs in various ways, such as spiritual manipulation or bullying, and for those with a history of abuse, it can reawaken those memories and the behaviour patterns we have developed to defend ourselves and be even more damaging. There were some things that have helped me, though. The passage of time is one – not by denying or burying the past, but recognising that what happened is a part of my history but not something that defines me. I have sought to process what happened in various ways, including receiving therapy. I talk my feelings out with others and I journal. I have had prayer for healing from within the Christian community.

In the end, bitterness will not help me or heal me: rather, it will paralyse me further. I stand at the foot of the cross knowing that God has forgiven me. So I will continue my journey to forgive others and so continue to walk on in the growing freedom that my friendship with Jesus brings me.

5

Discovering Love

God is love.[1]

John, apostle of Jesus

Hearing a Voice from the Past

I love Jesus. It really is that simple. He has changed my life.

Sometimes I look at children laughing in the market square and I find it hard to remember that I was like that once, but maybe I wasn't. Perhaps I've always been searching for love like a dying animal in the desert searches for water where no oasis can be found. Perhaps we are all searching for love, because however much or little love we have received from those who are meant to care for us, it can never quite be enough. I've come to believe that only God's love can fill that aching void.

What I do know is that I have always felt a little lost, as though something was missing at the very core of me. And I tried – oh, how I tried, at what cost – to find what it was, to fill the gap, but nothing worked, and the direction my life took as a result only led to a greater pain and loneliness than before. I became separated from others, scorned as being different when I'm not so very sure I was, but it is always easier to ostracise and pillory others than to look at any darkness within ourselves. Regardless of the opinion of others, my life was heading down a blind alley and I couldn't see any way for it to become any different.

At first, it was just a name I kept hearing. Yeshua.[2] The rescuer. At first I just gave a cynical smile. My life needed a liberator, but I took no notice, crawling dispiritedly from day to day. I kept hearing it though, again and again. Some people claimed he had healed them, others that he had released them from demons. For ages I resisted, and then curiosity overpowered even my scepticism and I figured I had nothing to lose. So the next time he was near our town (not that I felt it was 'ours', more the one I lived in), I decided to go and listen.

Skulking at the back of the crowd so as not to be seen, at first I was simply amazed at the number and variety of people that were there. Young and old, men and women, the rich and the impoverished, religious types and those like me who they would cross over the street to avoid. All of them hanging on his every word as though their lives depended on it.

In time I stopped my curious bystanding and began to actually listen to what he had to say. Almost at once I was drawn in. It wasn't just what he said, though that was astounding: he spoke about a God of love and mercy, a God who was like a rock we could build our lives on, a God who welcomed mixed-up, muddled people who knew they had messed up and wanted a new start. He said our lives could head off in the opposite direction from the track that we were on; God could turn them around; instead of worrying, we could trust, and our hearts mattered more to God than anything on the outside. I'd never heard anything like it.

But more than all that, incredible though the teaching was, it was something about him and the way he said it. I couldn't take my eyes off him. It was as if there was something completely different about him from any other man I had ever met. As if, were you to cut him through, what you would find would be love. Not some spurious sentiment but something tough and protective of the vulnerable, which looked for justice, that didn't pretend things were OK but accepted people as they were and offered something new. As I listened it was as though I was bathed in gentle, warm cleansing water and I realised perhaps even someone like me could start again.

So that day when I heard he was coming to Simon's house I had to go. I don't think I had really planned anything though I took the perfume with me. I think I just hoped to somehow say thank you. But then as I saw him, even though he was surrounded by people I knew would disapprove of me, I just had to approach him, and as the love erupted from my heart in an unstoppable flow, I could not control the tears. Every moment of heartbreak cascaded down my cheeks and poured on to his feet. It was as though every sordid mistake, every wrong turn, every image which came unbidden in the small hours was being washed away as each rivulet tracked down my careworn face.

I had to kneel. Not in submission, but in adoration. I took down my hair, barely registering the shocked gasps from the other men there, wiping my tears from his feet and joyously emptying out the perfume, knowing I was pouring out my heart to him as I did. I did not need to say anything, did not even need to look at his face, because I could sense his absolute tenderness as he accepted not just my gift, but me, all I had been, and was, but also could still be.

Yes, I love Jesus. It really is that simple. He has changed my life.

***

Luke 7:36–50 records this extraordinary story in these words:

[36] When one of the Pharisees invited Jesus to have dinner with him, he went to the Pharisee's house and reclined at the table. [37] A woman in that town who lived a sinful life learned that Jesus was eating at the Pharisee's house, so she came there with an alabaster jar of perfume. [38] As she stood behind him at his feet weeping, she began to wet his feet with her tears. Then she wiped them with her hair, kissed them and poured perfume on them.

[39] When the Pharisee who had invited him saw this, he said to himself, 'If this man were a prophet, he would know who is touching him and what kind of woman she is – that she is a sinner.'

[40] Jesus answered him, 'Simon, I have something to tell you.'

'Tell me, teacher,' he said.

[41] 'Two people owed money to a certain moneylender. One owed him five hundred denarii, and the other fifty. [42] Neither of them had the money to pay him back, so he forgave the debts of both. Now which of them will love him more?'

[43] Simon replied, 'I suppose the one who had the bigger debt forgiven.'

'You have judged correctly,' Jesus said.

[44] Then he turned towards the woman and said to Simon, 'Do you see this woman? I came into your house. You did not give me any water for my feet, but she wet my feet with her tears and wiped them with her hair. [45] You did not give me a kiss, but this woman, from the time I entered, has not stopped kissing my feet. [46] You did not put oil on my head, but she has poured perfume on my feet. [47] Therefore, I tell you, her many sins have been forgiven – as her great love has shown. But whoever has been forgiven little loves little.'

[48] Then Jesus said to her, 'Your sins are forgiven.'

⁴⁹ The other guests began to say among themselves, 'Who is this who even forgives sins?'

⁵⁰ Jesus said to the woman, 'Your faith has saved you; go in peace.'

The setting for this wonderful story is interesting, taking place at a meal Jesus attends in the house of a Pharisee. Much Christian teaching is too simplistic in its portrayal of the Pharisees. As human beings, we love to divide the world into 'goodies' and 'baddies'; it makes us feel secure: that the world can be understood and makes uncomplicated sense. This desire for simplicity has resulted in much teaching and preaching depicting the Pharisees as rigid legalists implacably opposed to Jesus, when a careful reading of the biblical account and better understanding of the background makes for a much more nuanced view.

The Pharisees were people of deep faith who sought to live holy lives. Their name means 'set apart'. They believed that God gave Moses the Law and the rest of the Torah.³ This, together with the Talmud which includes rabbinical discussion on the Law as well as the Law itself, laid out how people should live (whether Jews or those seeking to follow God by converting to Judaism). They also believed that these laws needed to be interpreted to help people understand how they applied to everyday life, and it is this development which led to various complex rules and the potential legalism which at times led to clashes with Jesus when the letter of the law, as later interpreted, conflicted with God's heart of compassion from which those same laws had been birthed. However, it is important not to lose sight of their desire to lead lives which pleased God and help others to do so. Clearly some Pharisees responded positively to Jesus, for example, Nicodemus.⁴

In this particular instance what we do know is that Simon, a Pharisee, had invited Jesus to eat with him. Jesus had accepted, despite the mixed reception he received from the religious leaders. He reached out to them as much as to those outside of religious systems and even, perhaps in particular, those excluded from normal society. We cannot be sure if this invitation came from genuine interest, or if Simon was a collector of celebrity guests, or if he wanted to find cause to oppose or correct Jesus. Jesus' words later[5] do make clear that, for whatever reason, Simon was not a good host, omitting many of the usual signs of hospitality a visiting rabbi might expect.

When any public figure was invited to a meal there was open access for the community to listen on the outskirts of the event, which this woman took much further by approaching Jesus where he was leaning at the low table to eat, as was their custom. Some commentators have assumed this is the same story as those describing an anointing of Jesus close to his death,[6] but anointing was common and this account is quite different.

This woman says nothing in her encounter with Jesus, at least in Luke's account, but her actions have extraordinary eloquence. We don't know why she had been branded '*a sinner*', although the usual assumption is sexual sin of some kind. However, it need not necessarily be the case – anyone whose lifestyle put them outside the laws as interpreted by the Talmud, including for example shepherds, could be branded sinners by the religious leaders. Jesus, though, refers to her '*many*' sins, so in whatever way, it does seem her life has gone badly wrong.

We don't know how or where she has encountered Jesus before, but clearly she has. Her behaviour towards Jesus as he reclines at the table, plainly motivated by deep love as Jesus later points out, was costly in every sense. If the perfume was nard, for example, it would have cost an average person's annual wage. If she was, as many assume, a prostitute, there is even more poignancy in the story since the perfume poured out would have been procured at great cost in the way she had earned it. If it was a dowry, which it could have been because some women carried their dowries in jars around their necks, pouring it out may have represented lost hope of a marriage because of her occupation as well as expressing her love for Jesus.

Overcome with emotion, she weeps, and the text says, with some decorum, that she wipes his feet with her hair, an action which would have necessitated letting it down. No respectable Jewish woman would ever do that in public. Initially, Luke describes her as standing at his feet, but she must have knelt to wash her tears from his feet with her hair. Again, if she was a prostitute, letting down her hair would have been a familiar action for her, but this would be the last time she would ever have to do it in that former way as she lived out her new, forgiven, life.

Simon is both stunned and scandalised, believing that such an action going unrebuked discredited Jesus' credentials as a prophet. In fact, the original language strongly suggests Simon did not believe he was. If Jesus were a godly man, surely he would not let her touch him, particularly in this intimate way? He does not voice these thoughts, but Jesus perceives them and tells him a story.

Jesus describes two debtors: one owing about two months' wages, the other nearer two years. Debt in the ancient world was potentially even more serious than it is now, and an even bigger issue. The one the debt is owed to has various actions open to him, but forgives both the debts. Jesus asks Simon a question, '*Now which of them will love him more?*' Simon replies, apparently grudgingly, '*I suppose the one who had the bigger debt forgiven.*' Jesus then points out that Simon has not even given him the normal courtesies as a host – no washing of feet (to wash off the grime from the dusty roads), no traditional kiss of greeting, no anointing of the forehead with a drop of incense or essential oil of roses. Yet this woman has literally lavished love upon Jesus in these extravagant ways. The clear implication is that she has discovered forgiveness and therefore her love is great, which Jesus then confirms. In contrast, Simon's love appears lacking – not, we may assume, because he has little to be forgiven, but because he does not realise his need for forgiveness. The link Jesus makes between forgiveness and love is significant and can be misunderstood. She loves because she has already been forgiven, rather than forgiveness being granted as a result of her expressing her love. Her joy at finding mercy has overcome the fear and risks of such a public display of adoration. Jesus, no doubt aware that her reputation would take some shaking off, makes a public declaration of her forgiveness, twice. She is free to live out her new life.

Jesus never saw leading a godly life as necessitating separation from those whose lives had taken a difficult and messy direction; quite the reverse. He sought them out, as they did him. He clearly saw people through the eyes of potential, envisaging all God had created them to be. He did not see the cleaning up of a person's life as a prerequisite of coming to him; rather, it was the natural result when they did.

In any potential criticism of the Pharisees, people of faith need to ensure that both in their individual lives and in churches they are not perpetuating similar attitudes, expecting people to live well (however that is defined) in order to be accepted, rather than themselves leading lives and building communities of welcome where people can discover God's love and its transforming power for themselves. In addition, there is a searching question: why is it that those outside religious circles were so drawn to Jesus, and yet many people today feel that they are not good enough or would not be welcome in a church? Equally, for those of us within churches, is it all too easy to lose sight of the need for forgiveness?

***

Let's hear another story of someone's search for love leading them to encounter Jesus . . .

Hearing a Voice from the Present

The thing that I remember most about my childhood is the loneliness and the fear. My parents had both mental health and substance abuse issues, in particular my father. They were not able to care for my brother and me, and so I simply never felt safe. I always had to put myself to bed at night – there were no bedtime stories or cuddles before sleep. From when I went to infant school at just 5 I had to take myself there and back, and I felt so very small in a very big world.

As a result I was always anxious, and that showed itself in so many ways. I would have nightmares: peculiar ones such as that I had to divide 3 by 10 exactly, and that if I didn't do so precisely I would float into space and be annihilated for ever. Looking back, I can see how they came from my feeling that I could never be protected and secure – there was no one to hold me (literally or metaphorically) and so anything could happen at any time.

There was no one in my life who I could trust. Now I know more, I realise that unlike most children, there were no attachment figures for me, who could help me to explore the world and give me that safe base to always come back to. I was adrift in a dangerous sea with no sense of a lifeboat that would ever come to my rescue.

There was one exception to this isolated and scary existence. Across the road was a godly woman who looked after me sometimes. She was a stable presence in my life and I am sure that she was praying for me. I suspect that has had a huge impact on me in many unseen ways.

As I grew older, the lack of a father figure who I could rely on to protect me led to me looking for love from other men. Somehow I knew they were not genuine, but I always felt I had to make do with whatever they offered, however unsatisfying and even damaging it might be. I struggled to feel I was worth anything and, in any case, I had no yardstick to measure what real love looked like. Somehow I always expected or hoped for too much, and so time and again I would be devastated when the love I was looking for was not there for me.

Eventually I did get married, though, and for a time things seemed a little better. However, just as our third child, a girl, was born, my husband simply left. I was alone again and with the responsibility of three young children when I felt I was still a child myself in so many ways, still looking for love and safety.

I had a series of relationships, again facing disappointment after disappointment and struggling to hold on to any sense of self-esteem. I hated seeing what I perceived as perfect families in church. Although I was a Christian and had been for some time, I felt as though I could never fit in – I was different, damaged and vulnerable. They seemed to have the wonderful life I craved. Churches can be healing places, but they can be lonely too.[7]

In time I married a kind man who had his own vulnerabilities as he was unwell. By now I was so wounded that I drank in his care for me. He cared for me and the children. I thought, naively perhaps, that God would not let anything more happen after everything else, but life is never that simple. Though my husband had never been fully well, he became much more ill, and an invalid, and I was back doing all the caring again.

This time I was angry, the flip side of my pain. I was livid with God. I'd only just about hung on to my faith through the years. I was furious with my husband, even though I knew he did not choose to be ill. Most of all, I was angry with myself, for all the choices I had made. The anger turned inwards to depression.

Initially I started drinking to escape into sleep – a kind of liquid anaesthetic to dull my pain and isolation. However, it escalated to a point where I knew I was losing control and so in time I joined AA.[8] There I found a supportive community – more so, sadly, than some of the churches I had been to which seemed (rightly or wrongly) full of people who had everything together and would be shocked by the reality of my life.

When I was at my most vulnerable, I met a man through my work as a teacher who showed me some attention. This encounter developed into a relationship and was to last for six years. I felt a terrible sense of guilt, at times enough to make me very depressed and self-destructive, but there were just moments when he held me and for a brief instant I felt loved and safe. There was a sense of connection too – we talked about everything in a way that was so easy and comfortable.

Yet I knew he was lying to me, and had partners in those years who he was lying to as well. It was as if I would put up with anything, however unsatisfactory and even wrong, for those small crumbs of affirmation and affection which, tiny as they were, surpassed anything that I had received from anywhere else.

Yet in all this I held on, however tenuously, to God. I really tried to stay close to him. I knew this was not his best for me, yet I also felt that he understood, more than anyone, including me, why my life had taken the direction it had. I often thought about the woman who anointed Jesus' feet and the love and acceptance she found from Jesus – he did not label her like everyone else did. After a while I began to pray, over and over again, for God to somehow take the decision out of my hands to end the relationship. I asked God to send his Holy Spirit to help me.

And God did. In a way I never expected, things came to a sudden end. I was relieved, but also found it incredibly painful. But God had answered my prayer and I was free. He had never condemned me. He knew I needed to be held and loved and, yes, I went about it the wrong way, but I do believe that God will be able to give me the deep acceptance and comfort – just in a way that will not harm me. In reality, he is the only one who can. His love and mercy are endless.

That woman who knelt at Jesus' feet poured out a lifetime of her hurt. She massaged his feet. I love what she did. It's safe to love Jesus. Even our most reliable people die, leave, or just can't help us as we need. I know that no one can replace the things I needed as a child, and at times that makes me very sad. I need God's love.

I don't know what my future will hold. I've since trained in health care so that I can give the gentle healing touch to others that I know I've needed. Perhaps I will always look for that father I never had. Maybe I will always love too much. I have no idea.

But that woman who was in so much pain found her way into history in God's book. She was not annihilated, forgotten or useless. Jesus loved her, and he loves me. God knew her story and he also knows mine. Her story has helped others, and I pray that mine can too.

I've learned a hard lesson, but I am keeping my bruised heart open for his healing oil to pour in.

Part 2

Challenges

6

Losing a Child

There's no tragedy in life like the death of a child.
Things never get back to the way they were.[1]
Dwight D. Eisenhower, US President

Hearing a Voice from the Past

I feel as though my heart has been ripped out. He is gone.

Sometimes, in my dreams, I go back to how it was. My body, after those first exhausting, nauseous weeks, beginning to blossom. The way I would hold my growing stomach, gently caressing it as though rehearsing for those times ahead when I would hold my newborn and gently stroke that baby-down hair. Reassuring them that I was here, that they were already loved. Those first fluttering sensations which it took me time to recognise as the movement of the new life I was growing and nurturing. And then the kicks, growing stronger, making me chuckle or startling me when they came unexpectedly, as though to remind me that yes, there was real life inside. Or the rhythm of the baby's hiccups. None of the women had told me about that. How they made me smile.

As the birth approached, of course I became nervous, even afraid. How would I cope? Would the baby be alright? Other women shared their stories with me, and whilst I enjoyed feeling part of this mysterious grouping 'mothers', their tales did nothing to allay my anxieties, rather adding to them with complications I had not yet thought of.

When the time came, the birth was difficult. The midwives were summoned with the birthing stool, one ready to clean and swaddle the baby, one to encourage and help me. It took a long time and at some moments I thought I might die. But then, just as I thought I could push no more, out he came, my beautiful boy, his cry heralding his entry into the world and the transformation of mine. I held him to my breast and I wept; relief and love intermingled as the tears coursed down my cheeks.

I loved those early days and weeks, showing him proudly to the women, feeding him with pride that not only had I given him life but I was still giving him my milk to help him grow. I watched him as he suckled, tiny hands curling around my finger, eyes holding my gaze as if as fascinated by me as I was by him.

He changed so much that first year. Rolling, then sitting, and finally crawling and walking. Sounds becoming the start of words with so much promise. I longed to teach him so many things. Beginning to eat our food, chewing a matzo, especially as his new teeth came. I would happily watch him, as I dreamed of the man he would become. Our community was small, but I knew others would take pleasure in watching him grow almost as much as we would. I was quietly contented.

There was no warning of the soldiers' coming. I heard the horses' hooves, but assumed it was a Roman legion passing through on the way to Jerusalem, or some of Herod's men en route to somewhere from Herodium. I disliked our not being a free nation, but aside from the ruthless taxes, in our quiet village I could try to distance myself from the occupying forces.

But then I heard a screaming, an almost animal sound as though some wild creature was being tortured. I rushed from the house, instinctively grabbing my son, to see a soldier stride from my neighbour's house, carrying her baby boy, just a newborn. She was shrieking at him to stop, to give him back, pawing futilely at him, but he was taking no notice, just shrugging her off. Later I wondered if what he was expressing really was indifference, or was actually distress. They usually fight men, not women and children – and some of them must be fathers too. I watched helplessly as another soldier came out of my friend's house, carrying both her sons, aged just a few months and nearly 2. She was running behind him, bewilderment etched on her face. Just then a third soldier saw me, shielding my precious toddler from the noise and distress, and as I saw him advance, I frantically looked around for shelter as my terror from this inexplicable invasion grew. But within two paces he was there, pushing me aside like a ragdoll. I have never felt so helpless, sobbing and begging for my son, yet knowing, seeing the stony face of the soldier, that any attempt to save him was useless. And soon all I could hear was the weeping of the women – mothers and grandmothers – and the agonised question floating in the air at the retreating backs: 'Why?' I was not even sure who I was asking the question of – the soldiers, or my God.

I would have died to save him.

And now I only wish I could.

My boy, my beautiful boy is gone. And my heart is broken beyond any repair.

***

This tragic story is from Matthew 2:13–18:

[13] When they [the Magi] had gone, an angel of the Lord appeared to Joseph in a dream. 'Get up,' he said, 'take the child and his mother and escape to Egypt. Stay there until I tell you, for Herod is going to search for the child to kill him.'

[14] So he got up, took the child and his mother during the night and left for Egypt, [15] where he stayed until the death of Herod. And so was fulfilled what the Lord had said through the prophet: 'Out of Egypt I called my son.'

[16] When Herod realised that he had been outwitted by the Magi, he was furious, and he gave orders to kill all the boys in Bethlehem and its vicinity who were two years old and under, in accordance with the time he had learned from the Magi. [17] Then what was said through the prophet Jeremiah was fulfilled:

[18] 'A voice is heard in Ramah,
weeping and great mourning,
Rachel weeping for her children
and refusing to be comforted,
because they are no more.'[2]

Although this appalling massacre is both in the gospel text and part of the church's year,[3] it seems to me that most churches ignore this disturbing story amid the Christmas celebrations. There is no 'deep and dreamless sleep'[4] in this brutal narrative. Indeed, some have doubted its historicity, pointing out that the Jewish historian Josephus does not mention it, despite his comments on a number of Herod's misdeeds.[5] They argue that Matthew is merely seeking to find the fulfilment of prophecy around the birth of Jesus.

However, I don't think we need to doubt this event just because, as well as recounting it, Matthew chooses to reflect theologically.[6] Though truly dreadful, it is numerically small compared to others of Herod's deplorable deeds – estimates of the number of babies and toddlers involved vary between twenty and thirty[7] – whereas some of his other atrocities saw hundreds murdered. He was clearly an insecure man who would do anything to preserve power if he suspected anyone of plotting against him. He even killed his wife Mariamne, his mother-in-law and two of his sons, Alexander and Aristobulus.

We may assume from the reference to the '*house*' earlier in verse 11 and the killing of children under 3 that these were not Jesus' newborn days, despite the popularity of kneeling Magi in crib scenes.[8] It would make sense that Mary and Joseph would have stayed for some time in Bethlehem after the birth, to allow for the various religious duties as well as allowing opportunity for recovery. Since the Magi saw the star at Jesus' birth, by the time they had made the journey, Jesus would no longer have been a newborn – the journey from their country of origin would have taken some time.

The poignant reference from Jeremiah[9] is telling. In Jewish life, Rachel was seen as the sorrowful mother, having died in childbirth.[10] She is one of many biblical women who suffer enormous pain and loss – beginning with the killing of Abel[11] by his brother Cain, surely ripping out Eve's heart. There are so many others – what about Rizpah, keeping lonely and heart-broken vigil over the bones of her sons, shaming the king until they were properly buried?[12] Stories of women encountering devastating loss continue right through the pages of the

Bible to Mary herself who is told by Simeon at Jesus' presenta-
tion in the Temple '*a sword will pierce your own soul*'.[13] Many
biblical women (and, of course, men) pay a price for the fulfilment of God's plan in Jesus: their stories finding their part in
God's bigger story, but their part not being forgotten.

In the time of Jeremiah, the captives would have trudged
wearily past Rachel's tomb, which was near Bethlehem, on
their way to the exile in Babylon, and Jeremiah is imagining
her bewailing this catastrophe even from her grave. It must
have seemed to that generation, defeated by war and scattered
by exile, that God had abandoned his people to their fate.
Matthew paints a powerful picture of the wailing and lamen-
tation echoing down through the centuries, sounds birthed in
terrible suffering.

Yet amid this indescribable suffering, the prophecy from
Jeremiah is not without hope. The context of the original is
of God bringing the exiles back – the next verse includes the
words '*they will return from the land of the enemy. So there is
hope for your descendants*'.[14] The whole of Jeremiah 31 sings
with promise. Deliverance will come. There is a rescuer. There
is still pain, but God in this child will in time deal the defin-
itive blow to death itself, not by violence but by the sacrifice
of his own life.

Nonetheless, the story remains as a disturbing reminder that
Jesus is born and grows amid great suffering and that the battle
with evil is all too real. Yet despite that, indeed because of it,
he is Immanuel, God with us.[15] God with us in the mess, the
muddle, the violence, the death and pain. There is nothing in
our lives from which he is remote or about which he does not
know. He weeps with us.[16]

***

Hearing a Voice from the Present

Is it possible to unbirth our children?

Is it possible that this period of unbirthing is a good gift that can lead to peace?

For nine months I'd carried him. Deep within. From flutters to tiny twists to fulsome turns, his movements offered precious months of intimacy even as I dreaded the delivery to come. My daily experience of the scarring pain of an earlier delivery reminded me that maybe these quiet nine months of anticipation would be the least painful of all those to come.

But he was born with such relative ease, labour lasting a few short hours. This gentle little one was calm, content, and sleeping in twelve-hour stretches at only 8 weeks. His growing exuberance for life, his abundant love for his two older sisters, his energy and optimism growing by the day, manifesting itself by the month and year, filling our home with life as we'd not quite experienced it before.

Gifted with passion and creativity, whatever he took on he approached with freshness. Following a script, fitting within perfect boundaries and neat lines, was not his approach. Perhaps that partially explains why he was misunderstood during some of his elementary school years. But he valued his home, cherished his sisters, wildly loved adventures with his dad, poured his heart and soul out to his grandparents, and nurtured close intimacy with me. We were the safe place from which an exciting world could be experienced.

He sought deep connection. Books and stories, read alone or shared aloud with parents and sisters, opened up other worlds and places, furnishing his mind with ideas for more and broader adventures. Music-making, studying, exploring and sharing his experiences gave harmonious, rich and resonant voice to emotions and insights he might not have otherwise expressed. The satisfying rewards of hard physical work, on construction site and golf-course green, were evident in his eyes, his biceps and his bounding nimble step.

Maybe it was that day in history class, early in his second high-school year, that changed everything. Maybe it changed nothing at all and was just the natural progression of his life story. Certainly it was a pivotal day.

It was the day a rather quiet girl – only newly arrived back in this county after three years of living on a medical mission with her family in Haiti – told her story. In the previous year, Haiti had experienced a deadly earthquake killing thousands and leaving thousands more in horrific circumstances. This girl, then only 13 herself, was handed newborn twins whose family had died. The orphanage was bursting and every able adult and child pitched in. For months this young girl fed, bathed, clothed and otherwise cared for these twins, giving them the life and being the family they needed. She told of the beauty of Haiti, the courage of Haitians, her love for the twins, and the difficulty of being back in her birth country sitting in a sterile high-school classroom.

Our 15-year-old boy, despite the books, stories and wilderness adventures, had never heard or imagined such a story. It gripped him as it gripped the entire class, first with silence, and then slowly, one by one, each spontaneously reached into their pockets and, almost as though in liturgical form, walked to their quiet classmate's desk and started placing bills and coins on her desk. 'How can I help?' our boy gently asked, as he slid $20 into her hand.

Several months later, almost without the teacher's guidance, a dozen or more of the students present in that classroom that day found themselves at that particular mission, at that particular orphanage in Haiti. For ten days they absorbed the unexpected beauty of the place, the joy of the healthy, vibrant twins. They walked into the mountains, played with village children, painted cement block homes, and praised God together in exuberant Creole worship.

And on the mission rooftop terrace at sunset one night, accompanied by the conversation and prayer of a former military man turned high school teacher, our boy forgave those who had misunderstood him in his childhood, and with characteristic enthusiasm — more muted now, and with mature insight — consciously stood on a new threshold in his life, asking God how he could serve him with all that he had and was.

Our son was now solidly certain about his desire to serve God with his life. His goal became figuring out what that would look like.

Upon returning home, he asked to give public testimony of his faith within his church community. Many friends and cousins came out that day to celebrate with us.

I shared an excited peace with our boy about this, content and thankful at the good gift being given to us as we entered this new phase of our son becoming a man.

Mid-summer arrived. And with it, a few quiet days with grandparents at the family cottage.

Breakfast. Conversation. Swim. Lunch. Nap. Water-ski. And then.

Has anyone seen our boy?

No, seriously, has anyone seen him?

Actually, can you go and check his bedroom?

Actually, check all the bedrooms.

Oh. There are his sandals. Hmm. He left his phone on his bed. Wonder where he is.

Can someone check the . . .

Helicopters. Neighbours. Boats. Then fewer boats. Questions. Answers. Phone calls. People.

Then silence.

Five and a half hours pass.

The police officer asks us into the living room. I hear the sound of window blinds being lowered. She adjusts her heavy belt. I notice her gun and her strength. We are all standing – grandparents, parents, a sister. She looks into my eyes. And then says, 'The divers have found your boy. They are with his body on the other side of the lake. I am so sorry. My condolences.'

The ghastly phrase. 'My condolences.' Words that have never been said to me before. Words I cannot absorb. I will not absorb. Those words are not meant for me. My life does not need condoling.

And then the piercing sound, unlike anything I've heard before or since, shreds the air of the cottage. Our younger daughter, in the blossoming beauty of her life, wails in horror.

Wild wailing. Desperate sobs. Shrieking sorrow. Heaving shoulders. Swallowed howling marks the night. So many people sleeping – no, not sleeping at all – spread all over the cottage and on the dock trying to make it to morning, while this unknown noise, this crying and gnashing, knifes the darkness.

Dawn brings no relief. Only merciless light exposing exhausted deep stares between all those too tired to make more sound. A new weight settles itself on us, pressing unrelentingly.

Our boy. Our life. Our hope. Our music. Our joy. Our exuberant God-lover, people-carer. Smothered. Silenced. Gone.

Haunted, oppressed, horrified, dragging our new burden after us, on us, within us, we make our way home. Empty. Silenced.

Heavy stillness envelopes our life.

Loved-ones breathe for us.

Think for us.

Pray for us.

Make decisions for us.

Prop us up.

Say words to us.

Say words for us.

Sorrow and sighing attend our days.

Weeping and great mourning visit our nights.

We only want to curl up. Cover ourselves. Be alone. But not be alone. Talk. But not talk.

We want each day to end by 6:30, but force ourselves to stay up till 8:30. And then begin the hours of closing our eyes and seeing only, nothing but, our beautiful boy in his last horrible lonely minutes. We try to keep our eyes open to keep the visions away. The hole in my stomach, or is it my uterus, becomes bigger. It gnaws with blackness.

Yet somehow, slowly, the days pass. We make it through.

Minute by minute. Hour by hour. Day by day.

Weeks begin to unfold.

We dress. We drive. We work. We study.

We read. We sit. We pray.

We sigh. We are mostly rather still.

As we absorb this terrible thing that has entered our lives.

And yet we do not rage. We wonder at the incredible gift that has been given to us, the gift of the sure knowledge of our boy's love for God, his security in being forgiven, his own peace at forgiving.

As the weeks and months slowly began to pass, we realise that no horror in this shocking death is worse than that raw aching pain of the first months. I realise, with some surprise, that after nine months, almost to the day, the black aching gnawing piercing hole deep inside me seems to be gone. I realise it is not my constant companion and no longer is every moment marked by thoughts of our boy and his tragic death (a cardiac event, we are eventually told).

Is it possible that it takes nine months to unbirth one's child? What is it about the initial period of nine months that God has ordained for the growing of an unborn one? Surely, if not only a physical time, but also a period of deep emotional preparation for the parents, then, I wonder, when untimely death rips a child from this life, are these first nine months a period, not of growth and preparation, but of healthy surrender and release?

Indeed, our sorrow has slowly become marked by peace, by a deep and quiet thanksgiving for the good that Haiti and Haitian friends offered to our loved boy, by a sure knowledge that our loved son's death is known to God, that our cherished, exuberant boy is known to God. That one day we will be resurrected and be together again in the pure and beautiful embrace of the loving light of our heavenly Father, our Father who knows and was present that day and through all the days of our boy's life here on earth.

7

Overcoming Shame

*Shame. That horror that washes over you in
the middle of the night as your mind replays a
memory you desperately wish you could erase.*

Jeannie Kendall

Hearing a Voice from the Past

It's so easy to point the finger, isn't it? To glory in a smug, secure
self-righteousness as we watch someone else fall catastrophi-
cally from grace . . .

Not that I was thinking of anyone else when it happened.
I don't know if you can even begin to imagine. Yes, of course
at times I knew what we were doing was wrong. But there was
such an ache in the depths of my soul, and for a few moments
at least, especially as I was held when he was satiated, I could
almost persuade myself that I was loved. I felt, however briefly,
less alone.

And it was like that at the moment they came. I was wrapped
in his arms, dreaming, however pointlessly, of what could have
been if things were different, when they burst in, screaming
vile, shocking names, dragging me roughly by my arm out of

the house. I barely had time to grab my outer robe and drape it around me. I was shivering in shock, fear and humiliation. They just left him there. I never got to see the expression on his face, to know what he felt as I was hauled away.

I had no idea at first where they were taking me. I was gazing down, trying to keep from stumbling as they pulled me along. A trial? A stoning with no opportunity for defence? I felt hostile eyes despising me, though whether that was my imagination I didn't know. With each step I retraced my sorry life . . . not just all I had done, but who I had become. Did those foul names they were screeching really sum up who I was?

Then suddenly we stopped. I toppled over, exhausted, in the dust. The sand in my eyes and the myriad unspoken emotions brought tears, which I felt trickling down my cheeks and saw spilling on the ground, as I feared my blood soon would. I could only see the man's feet, encased in sandals, but he seemed young. They pulled me up to stand, but I still looked down. I felt utterly abandoned and desolate.

They asked him what to do with me, reminding him of the law, and so I realised he must be a rabbi. Any tiny shred of hope evaporated. Abject, I waited for him to say yes, stoning was the right thing. The just thing. I would have prayed but I had no words left, and anyway, I believed I had squandered any chance of God's compassion. Instead I tortured myself with futile questions. Who would miss me? How would they talk about me when I was dead? I had left no mark on the world. I was a nobody. A nothing.

But to my astonishment he didn't say anything at first. Instead, he bent down, even lower than me, writing something in the dust. I couldn't see what he wrote, but I assumed it was my penalty. I shut my eyes and tried to escape to a place of refuge inside my head while they carried on, savouring a brief moment of relief that their interrogation was for him, not me.

Then I sensed movement, and finally he spoke. '*Let any one of you who is without sin be the first to throw a stone at her.*' I flinched. It was about to begin. Now terror replaced my humiliation. More movement and I recoiled. But no stone came. More movement. As much from a need to know than from any hope, I opened my eyes. Still looking down, I saw that it was my accusers who were moving. Walking away. Confused, I watched their retreating feet.

But he was still there, and finally I looked up and met his eyes. Even now I can't describe what I saw there. It was as though I was utterly uncovered, but somehow in a different way to anything I had known before. He could see behind who I was, comprehending so much more than the broken woman standing in front of him. Yes, the mess and the wrong steps, but also the longing, and the need, and the desperate loneliness. He wasn't excusing, he was understanding. And more than that. It mattered . . . I mattered. And for the first time he spoke to me, his voice strong with authority yet as gently probing as his gaze. '*Woman, where are they? Has no one condemned you?*' I looked around, almost afraid to speak the words lest they return. '*No one, sir,*' I mumbled. He spoke again. '*Then neither do I condemn you . . . Go now and leave your life of sin.*'

And that was it. I was free to go. And more than that, so much more. I was free to live. Something in his understanding and acceptance of my broken self meant that I could start again.

I later expressed it this way . . .

I had lost all fight
Before they picked up stones.
More exposed there, clothed
Than ever I had been naked;

Seeing the hatred
In their eyes
I knew they were somehow
Stoning something in themselves.
Easier to call me an adulteress
Than see me
As a woman
Seeking some comfort
The only way she knew
When life had crushed
All dreams and hopes.

And then I saw him.
Such difference in his eyes.
Understanding was there
Though no excuses
Seeing past
All shame and regret
To what I could have been.
And could be still.

In the end, I fell *into* grace.

***

Let's look at the story as we have it recorded in John 7:53 – 8:11:

[53] Then they all went home, [1] but Jesus went to the Mount of Olives.

[2] At dawn he appeared again in the temple courts, where all the people gathered round him, and he sat down to teach them. [3] The teachers of the law and the Pharisees brought in a woman caught

in adultery. They made her stand before the group ^{4} and said to Jesus, 'Teacher, this woman was caught in the act of adultery. ^{5} In the Law Moses commanded us to stone such women. Now what do you say?' ^{6} They were using this question as a trap, in order to have a basis for accusing him.

But Jesus bent down and started to write on the ground with his finger. ^{7} When they kept on questioning him, he straightened up and said to them, 'Let any one of you who is without sin be the first to throw a stone at her.' ^{8} Again he stooped down and wrote on the ground.

^{9} At this, those who heard began to go away one at a time, the older ones first, until only Jesus was left, with the woman still standing there. ^{10} Jesus straightened up and asked her, 'Woman, where are they? Has no one condemned you?'

^{11} 'No one, sir,' she said.

'Then neither do I condemn you,' Jesus declared. 'Go now and leave your life of sin.'

There is a bit of a puzzle around this text. The earliest manuscripts do not have this section, though later ones do, and a few manuscripts include some or all of the story in other places, such as Luke's gospel.^{1} Certainly if it was originally in Luke's gospel it would fit well with his interest in people (and specifically outsiders), but it seems to me to have the marks of authenticity here too. It fits exactly with the picture of Jesus we have in all four gospels. When questioned in the Temple, for example,^{2} he is skilled at turning the question back to the questioners, and his compassion for ordinary, damaged people is consistent in the stories about him. There is another good argument for this story belonging here. As Tom Wright points out,^{3} in John 7 Jesus has been teaching in the Temple and there seems to be genuine interest in all that he is saying. However, John 8 has a much more negative feel, with some very severe words from Jesus, and ends with these sinister words: *'At this, they picked up stones to stone him, but Jesus hid himself, slipping away from the temple grounds.'* It seems as though something has happened. Whilst chapter 8 is full of radical claims by Jesus, which would have been considered blasphemous, it is possible that this story is also part of the explanation. From wanting to stone her, they now want to stone him.

Commentators often highlight, rightly, the absence of the man in this story. Is he taking any responsibility? What this woman has done is only part of the story, and the fact that she is the one dragged out and humiliated certainly reflects the patriarchy of the day as well as, perhaps, the attitude of the men using her as a pawn to trap Jesus. She is caught in a story not of her choosing, but a story which ultimately God can use so that she might be free to write her own, new, chapter as well as giving fresh hope to others.

Jesus' bending down and writing in the ground with his finger has also birthed much speculation. What did he write? Was it something to help her, and in any case, could she have seen it through her tears, her eyes lowered with shame? Was he buying time to think? Or scribbling, in contempt at their hypocrisy? We don't know, of course, though it is fascinating to imagine. What impacts me more, though, is that Jesus deliberately chose not to tower over her, emphasising their differences, but to stoop down to her level: a specific example of his entire life stance as he *'set aside the privileges of deity and took on the status of a slave, became* human . . . *an incredibly humbling process.'*[4]

With piercing insight, Jesus challenges her sanctimonious indicters. They can stone her – it's the law – but only if they can declare themselves innocent. Did he list their sins, their moments of private disgrace, in the dust? Or was his astute and unrelenting gaze enough? Whatever the cause, they slink away, leaving her alone with Jesus and awaiting, surely, the pain from the first rock from the only guiltless man, the one person entitled to throw it.

He doesn't, of course. Condemnatory stone-throwing has never been Jesus' approach. Instead he releases her, offering the possibility of a life she has not yet known. She is tenderly handed a freedom she could never have envisaged in that terrifying moment of capture.

The reality, surely, is that we all have moments like this. Instances about which, when we remember them, the creeping heat of shame comes over us: when we wish more than anything that our lives were like computer files which could be deleted – whether a brief, even petty, moment hardly enough to register as a bit or nibble, or in contrast vast yottabytes of memory. Times which still flash through our consciousness, unbidden and unwelcome, in the midnight waking hours when we feel most alone as we assume the world around us sleeps in apparent tranquillity.

Just as for this unnamed woman, it is still possible to find that, as we tell our stories, God's grace can bring us freedom from our shame.

***

Our human capacity for sexual failure, and God's ability to deal with our resulting shame, continues today. Let's hear another story . . .

Hearing a Voice from the Present

I wish I could be clear about when it started. Looking back, that time in my life is like a fog, curling around my life and memory. It is easy to make excuses. I was exhausted, from a demanding job in social care. Around me there was nothing but need and, at times, despair, and I so often felt powerless to help, other than to put a few protocol-bound sticking plasters over gaping life-wounds. I had refused to listen to my body, screaming at me as it was that I needed to rest, a persistent headache my constant companion.

Home, too, was demanding. Two small children and a perpetually exhausted wife perhaps exacerbated the usually insignificant minor differences and birthed the ability to lose each other in the mundane, a risk which lurks even in the most successful of relationships. Who knows? What I do know is I felt lonely, with a childish resentment that no one appeared to be thinking about me, or what I needed.

And then I met her. She was new in the office and at first I simply sought to be a good colleague, to make her welcome. Initially I thought nothing of the innocuous joking, the shared smiles over the peculiarities of our co-workers. I barely registered that I was looking out for her when I first got in, ignored the warning twinge of disappointment if she wasn't there. I was running full speed towards a cliff and was blind to everything but my own fragile ego which was being boosted by what I saw simply as an innocent friendship. In retrospect, my naivety was breath-taking.

The turning point came when we had to work together on a complex case. We drove a lot of miles together, sharing stories as the emotional intimacy silently grew. I told her things about myself, my formative years, secret hopes and fears, that I had never told anyone, not even my more pragmatic wife. She listened, really listened. She reciprocated, and I felt important, the holder of her secrets. I can see now, with the luxury of looking back, that we were really two needy children, who for different reasons had never really addressed the chasm of poverty within, instead sublimating it by giving to others the care we had never received. But hindsight, of course, gives a twenty-twenty vision which is unobtainable in ordinary life.

As we bathed unknowingly in the glow of mutual affection, suddenly and shockingly the client we were working with died. However professional we are, we are not immune from human emotions, and we had both cared about her. We were alone in the office when the call came. She took it, and as her face became ashen I knew something was very wrong. As she blurted out the news, tears streaming down her face, unthinkingly I drew her to me for what I had intended as a comforting hug. I believe the die was cast in that moment.

Days later we were on a conference, and the emotional intimacy drifted into physical. It was never really only about sex. It was about the longing for connection with another person, which I had lost. About feeling I was important, which deep down perhaps I had never felt. It was about many things, a chasing after a nameless something as elusive and unobtainable as the wind.

There were moments of regret – such as coming home, with the memories of stolen moments still fresh, to three pairs of trusting eyes, oblivious then to my betrayal. I rationalised it, skilfully telling myself untruths that brushed the guilt away. No one was being hurt, and I was simply meeting a need. Surely that would make me a more empathic worker, a better husband and father?

Until my flimsily built house of cards came toppling down. Thinking that we were alone, an office door opened and at the same time, the door on that relationship closed. Frightened at the implications, my friend sold me out, creating a story which perhaps she could use to assuage her own guilt, but which made me the villain of the piece. My line manager, thinking it a kindness, sent me home to seek help for what she saw as a stress-related aberration of character. That in turn raised so many questions that eventually I broke down and told my wife everything. She was devastated.

Even beginning to describe those feelings still brings uncomfortable waves of emotion. I know I won't drown in them now, but the sensation is still painful. Apparently it is a common dream that we are walking down the street only to discover we are naked. That is exactly how I felt, except during daylight. I felt exposed, vulnerable and utterly ashamed. I could barely sleep, but when I did, blissfully unaware for a brief spell, I would wake in a cold sweat, fear for the future prickling my skin. At other times when I woke, it was as if it had not happened and then as sleep slipped away, the horror returned in a rush. I was also indescribably hurt by what I saw as the betrayal of my friend. I had trusted her with my secrets, laid myself bare literally and metaphorically, and she had, it seemed, thrown it all in my face, exposing me to the judgement of my colleagues. Looking back, I realise she was fighting for survival in her own way, but it cut very deep. The perceived derision of others somehow struck at the very root of who I was. Was I that person they now saw me to be? Did what I had done define for all time who I was? At times I wanted to die, but even this choice somehow was denied as I felt obliged to carry on, to try to appease, make something right. If I had felt alone before the affair, now I felt utterly abandoned, alone in a desolate wilderness of my own making. I have no idea how I kept going, smiling day after day for the clients, looking as if everything was normal at work where most of the staff were blissfully unaware.

In time I moved on at work and rebuilt things at home, even stronger than before in many ways. But the sense of shame lingered at the very depths of my soul. Sometimes it would just wash over me again, unbidden. I covered it over, making my mark at the new job and making strenuous efforts at home. Yet the veneer seemed to me to be paper-thin. I reran memories of my humiliation in the small hours when sleep still evaded me. I was guarded at work, determined neither to trust nor self-disclose ever again.

At around this time, my wife and I started to attend church, mainly for the children. I went through the motions, but my heart was not in it. I related to Adam and Eve, trying to vainly cover themselves after tasting the forbidden fruit which seemed so sweet, only to turn into bitter ash. The idea of God frightened me – surely he would see who I was and judge me even more than others? So mostly I didn't listen too carefully. I smiled, but let no one and nothing past my well-practised mask.

And then, one Sunday as the church made its way through the Gospel of John, we arrived at the story of the woman taken in adultery. At first I wanted to run. Surely, even in the reading of the story, my secret shame would be revealed? Would everyone turn to look at me, these (I assumed) good people who could never imagine the ravages of guilt I dragged there with me every week? Yet for the first time, hearing that story, I related to the Bible. I felt I knew how that unnamed woman felt, the horror and humiliation of exposure. Distracted briefly by my identification with her, I tried to listen more carefully. As I did so, I was astounded. I imagined myself there in her place and, as I did so, realised that this Jesus I had been studiously avoiding any encounter with might actually treat me with compassion; might find a way to reach me, help me rebuild my shattered self-image in the light not of my failure but of his love.

It is a long road, and I'm not there yet. But when the shame comes again, I imagine him writing my failure in the dust and then rubbing it away. I hear him say to me too '*neither do I condemn you*'.

In the end, like that woman, step by step I am being freed from my shame to live a new life.

8

Facing Long-term Illness

The question is not how to get cured, but how to live.[1]

Joseph Conrad

Hearing a Voice from the Past

I think it is probably very hard for most of you to imagine. It is certainly very hard for me to explain.

Thirty-eight years. So many Pesach, Shavuot and Sukkot pilgrimages where all I could do was watch others making their way to the Temple where I felt excluded. So many days, months, years, dragging out one after the other, each the same, one grey dawn after another, bringing no respite.

At the beginning, of course, I had hope. Illnesses are usually transient, and I expected this to be the same, a minor inconvenience but nothing that need be other than a trifling irritation before my life resumed its familiar pattern of caring for those around me, making a living, the daily chores. Even as I weakened, I still expected recovery, but as the days drifted to weeks and months, the reality began to creep up on me like a thief and to terrify me.

Most people were kind, but I felt as though I were a charity case, part of their Tzedakah, a religious duty for which I was a useful recipient. I could see the look of pity in their eyes and the relief that they were well and healthy, mixed with a little fear that this could happen to them too. Then there were the pious ones, who quoted me the Torah and asked me what sin I needed to repent of to get well. For a time I did torment myself with that, but in the end I decided if their God had something in mind, he needed to tell me.

When they began to carry me each day to the pool of Bethesda, I wasn't sure whether to be grateful or to feel as though they were taking me there to discharge their responsibility for me. Bethesda was a curious place to be. It was in so many ways dispiriting, surrounded by people for whom life was diminished: those for whom life was constant darkness, those whose limbs had betrayed them. Yet there was always the smallest glimmer of hope: as the waters were occasionally stirred it was said that the first into the water would find healing. So we all waited and watched, optimism constantly wrestling with despondency.

As months passed, though, this daily ritual became just another side to my desolation. The pool would occasionally stir, and I would struggle to move, my weakened limbs desperately sluggish despite the urges of my mind, willing my body to do my bidding. It was all so futile. Someone always got there first and my hope for ever finding healing slowly ebbed away. Resentment was always lurking closely – towards those who could get there, and in particular aimed at the God who had allowed this, and – some continued to tell me – caused it because of my wrongdoing. Still, I went each day, the people around me becoming companions in suffering; it was a relief to be with others who understood, rather than with those whose very normality separated them from me. With my limited vista I knew every scratch on those colonnades, each dent. Every day the same outlook.

Until that day. Another Sabbath, the way I counted off the interminable and indistinguishable weeks. My friends had again carried me there, arguing that they sought to both exercise compassion and potentially save my life, so no regulations were broken. I laid there, waiting to again count the hours. Even if the waters stirred, all that would happen would be that I would be stepped over (maybe even trodden on) yet again, ignored in the rush of others.

As I looked again at the waters, a shadow crossed my face and I realised that someone was standing there scrutinising me. Initially I was irritated – why did this stranger, who could walk and choose where to go and what to do, feel he could interrupt me when I could not move away? When he spoke, though, I was no longer annoyed but astounded. '*Do you want to get well?*' Anger welled up and I could not speak, but in the silence thoughts jumbled, fighting to reach expression. 'You fool! What do you think? That I chose to be here? That I like this? What are you saying? That I don't try hard enough to get into the water?' Somehow I managed to reply, hearing myself voice the helplessness I felt: '*I have no one to help me into the pool when the water is stirred. While I am trying to get in, someone else goes down ahead of me.*' He held my gaze for a long moment and, though I remained bewildered, the anger melted away as I sensed that somehow he understood. Who was this man?

To this day I don't understand why his next, absurd, words did not evoke anger or ridicule in me. '*Get up! Pick up your mat and walk.*' I opened my mouth to speak, but he continued to hold my gaze. For reasons I have never understood, I found myself reaching for his hand. Still maintaining eye contact,

I allowed him to raise me to my feet, and as I did so, I felt my weakness melt away like night mists in the morning sun. Strength was returning and so, almost dream-like, I picked up the pallet I had lain on, worn and faded by years of use, and walked away. I scarcely knew what I was doing, but my first steps for thirty-eight years turned out to be walking straight into a rebuke for carrying my mat – forbidden on the Sabbath. All I could say was that I'd been told to by the man who had made me well – but, of course, they wanted to know who, and I had no idea who he was. It hadn't occurred to me to ask amid the disorientation – or perhaps more realistically, the reorienta-tion – of my encounter with him.

My first instinct was to head to the Temple. For the first time in years I could worship with others. As I prayed, I felt the gen-tle presence of God, yet with a jolt realised that it was the same feeling I had experienced in the encounter with the stranger.

I suppose it should not have surprised me that he came to find me in the Temple. Even his words that held a warning were gentle. What I heard, tenderly spoken, was: 'You're not just physically healed, you are new. Live out your new life as you should.'

And I will. Meeting Jesus has made all the difference.

***

His story is found in John 5:1–15:

Some time later, Jesus went up to Jerusalem for one of the Jewish festivals. [2] Now there is in Jerusalem near the Sheep Gate a pool, which in Aramaic is called Bethesda and which is surrounded by five covered colonnades. [3] Here a great number of disabled people used to lie – the blind, the lame, the paralysed.[2] [5] One who was there had been an invalid for thirty-eight years. [6] When Jesus saw him lying there and learned that he had been in this condition for a long time, he asked him, 'Do you want to get well?'

[7] 'Sir,' the invalid replied, 'I have no one to help me into the pool when the water is stirred. While I am trying to get in, someone else goes down ahead of me.'

[8] Then Jesus said to him, 'Get up! Pick up your mat and walk.' [9] At once the man was cured; he picked up his mat and walked.

The day on which this took place was a Sabbath, [10] and so the Jewish leaders said to the man who had been healed, 'It is the Sabbath; the law forbids you to carry your mat.'

[11] But he replied, 'The man who made me well said to me, "Pick up your mat and walk."'

[12] So they asked him, 'Who is this fellow who told you to pick it up and walk?'

[13] The man who was healed had no idea who it was, for Jesus had slipped away into the crowd that was there.

[14] Later Jesus found him at the temple and said to him, 'See, you are well again. Stop sinning or something worse may happen to you.' [15] The man went away and told the Jewish leaders that it was Jesus who had made him well.

Jesus is at Jerusalem for one of the three major festivals: Passover, Pentecost and the Feast of Tabernacles. John does not tell us which, and Jesus appears to be alone as there is no mention of the disciples in this section. (The implication is that John heard the story later from Jesus himself or someone else.) Jesus visits this well-known place of healing, near the Temple Mount.[3]

Water was often considered sacred and was hugely significant in a land where it was precious and drought common. It is, of course, an eloquent symbol – it can be welcome, representing quenching of thirst or gentle cleansing, or powerful and frightening, such as an uncontrollable torrent of floodwater. John's gospel uses the imagery of water in a number of ways.[4] This particular pool – the original Greek word tells us it was a deep one – had disturbances, perhaps from an underground stream, around which a belief in healing at those times had arisen. It is possible that this was a sacred site for pagans as well as Jews.[5]

Something draws Jesus to this particular man – we don't know if he was told how long he had been an invalid or not. Having been ill for decades, the man was presumably not young and would have been physically atrophied as well as (we might assume) emotionally fragile, having long since given up hope. He has not requested anything of Jesus – indeed, we discover he does not know who he is – and Jesus seems to expect no faith from him, taking the initiative to relieve his suffering.

'*Do you want to get well?*' seems an odd question. The usual interpretation is that to find healing would mean big changes for this man, such as taking responsibility again and earning a living, and that perhaps this would be challenging for him as his illness has become a settled way of life. Whilst that is a possibility, I'm not sure that is the only way to hear the question, and that particular reading of it perhaps reflects our difficulty in dealing with long-term illness which tempts us, even now, to want to put blame somewhere or cast doubt on conditions we don't understand. Less pejoratively, the question may have been to raise hope where perhaps after decades it had been lost – Jesus is saying, in essence: 'Healing is possible, if you want it.' The man's response, still focused on the pool, is that it simply is not possible. At this point he does not seem to see Jesus as being able to heal him.

Jesus says, '*Get up!*' – literally, 'Be resurrected'. What he is offering is a totally new life.

He is asking the man to do the impossible – for decades he has been the one being carried, not doing the carrying. Yet, for whatever reason, he does not object but does indeed get up, finding healing as he acts on the word of Jesus. There is an interesting principle at work here about our need to cooperate with God whenever he is at work.

The Jews – we can assume just some of them – are scandalised. It was forbidden to carry anything on the Sabbath, not by the Old Testament scriptures, but by the Mishnah, the commentary on them, which gave thirty-nine classifications of work not permitted on the Sabbath, including carrying anything, except for compassionate reasons, in particular to save life.

Jesus finds him in the Temple – a seeking out reminiscent of the good shepherd searching for the one sheep in Luke 15. He seems to want to make sure complete healing takes place. He warns him not to sin, in case something worse happens. This raises the complex issue of the link between sin and sickness, which has caused not just controversy, but distress to many people. Just a few simple thoughts here:

Jesus clearly did not think sin always causes illness,[6] rather seeing sickness as an opportunity for God to work. Whilst it is a reality that some sustained damaging lifestyle choices impact on health, it should never be our assumption that the person is to blame for their illness if we seek to be loving followers of Jesus. It is not unusual for that assumption to be an underlying attitude in the person themselves, indicated by comments like: 'Why is God punishing me?' or 'What have I done to deserve this?' The gospels suggest other reasons for illness, including spiritual oppression, emotional issues such as forgiveness and, at times, no obvious reason at all. Those involved in praying for others need to exercise great caution – so much damage can be done to someone who is already suffering, by suggesting it is their fault in some way.

I think rather that Jesus is making clear to this man in their second encounter that he wants to bring wholeness, not just physical healing. He can not only give the physical life which the pool tantalised but never delivered – he also offers wholeness, *shalom*. He is not patching up a life, but offering an entirely new one. Arguably the man could have waited one day longer after all that time, and Jesus clearly chose to heal him on the Sabbath. The healing on the Sabbath, with its association of rest after creation, reminds Jesus' critics that God is bringing in a new creation, fulfilling all that was promised and making clear that compassion supersedes slavish law-keeping.

We are told that after Jesus has identified himself to the man, he tells the Jewish leaders (who had earlier asked him Jesus' identity) that it was Jesus. We cannot guess the man's motivation – it could easily have been not fearfully defending himself or even betrayal (as some suggest[7]), but instead the desire to let it be known what Jesus has done, which so many others in the gospels who were healed or witnessed healing exhibit,[8] particularly as, unlike the religious leaders, he emphasises the healing not the offence of bed-carrying. We simply don't know and I don't believe that descriptions of him as 'unattractive'[9] are fair on the evidence we have.

There are some scholars who see this story as allegorical:[10] the five porches representing the five books of the law (revealing sin but unable to heal), the thirty-eight years either the wilderness wandering or the number of centuries waiting for the Messiah, and the stirring of the waters representing baptism. Whilst John often uses symbolism, and such a meaning is possible – the Bible is full of deeper levels – this story stands in its own right as an example of Jesus' gracious compassion and the possibility of hope in even the longest of dark nights.

***

Even when healing does not come, the awareness of God's presence can make a difference. Here is another story:

Hearing a Voice from the Present

Living with a chronic illness, in my case, myalgic encephalomyelitis, or ME, is frustrating, exhausting and debilitating. It has made me functionally disabled, weak and more tired than I ever thought possible. Fractured sleep offers no relief. Light, sound and language are overwhelming, so much so that I have earplugs in most of the time. I cannot manage visitors or conversations for more than a few minutes and am so weak I cannot bathe on my own and have to use a plastic cup to drink from. Headaches, IBS and muscular pain are companions who rarely give me any peace.

This illness has taken everything I thought I knew and turned it upside down. In some ways it has made me a shell of my former self, and yet also, by God's grace, I have grown a new self within that is perhaps more vibrant and full of colour than who I was before I became ill, more than twenty-five years ago.

It all began with contracting the Epstein Barr virus (a form of glandular fever), when I was 19. A cycle began of periods of wellness interspersed by months of a horrible aching, fluey tiredness. I just about managed to finish my degree and start a job, and then a few things happened all at once: a personal trauma; overwork; flu and a fumigation of my flat. Somehow, one or all of these factors served to change the nature of the recurrent virus and suddenly I could barely function. I ended up on sick leave, thinking I needed a few weeks' rest, and haven't been able to work now for more than two decades.

A relapse in 1998 meant I could no longer walk more than around one or two rooms, and not manage stairs. I now live in a very small bungalow, and use a wheelchair on the rare occasions I'm able to go out. Today, as I write, I'm struggling against a headache, dreadful neck and shoulder pain, brain fog (inability to concentrate) and post-exertional malaise – exhaustion and aches in my muscles because I went out yesterday for the first time in four months, just for a short wheel around a playing field three minutes away by car. It was all I could manage, and that has to go down as a triumph. That's one thing about being chronically ill. Every small achievement is wondrous.

Those of us who suffer with debilitating illness have the opportunity to register gratitude and praise for things most people take for granted: brushing one's teeth unaided, sitting up in a chair for ten minutes. Thankfulness and wonder need to be constructed from the smallest things: a cup of tea; birds at the feeder outside the window; patterns of light coming through the curtains. For most sufferers (and our carers) there are no holidays, no daytrips, no weekend visits, just the same routine day in, day out.

The severity of ME[11] varies enormously between sufferers, and even from week to week. Any effort expended, whether physical, mental or emotional, takes its toll, usually after a day or so, and the pain and exhaustion last far longer than the activity did. In a better phase, I may have been able to have a drink with a friend in a quiet pub, but I suffered horribly afterwards when alone.

So, when you are chronically ill, you have to be good at pacing and planning. Spontaneity tends to fall by the wayside. There are lots of days, swathes of time even, when it feels like there is less than nothing to work with, as though we are a car limping from petrol station to petrol station, getting only a few drops of fuel to work with. Some of the latest research suggests that our energy is depleted on a cellular level, our bodies being simply unable to produce it.

But the effects of a long-term illness with no cure are not only the pain, dysfunction and horrible symptoms that sufferers experience in their bodies, they also reach into every area of life you can think of. All relationships alter or suffer. People find the change in us and our inability to take part too much to bear. When you cannot do normal things, people tend to drift away. Often, they just don't know how to relate to sickness or disability. Others are frightened by it.

My family have been supportive, but some people find even their close relatives are dismissive and impatient with a seemingly never-ending and never stabilising condition. Regarding ME, some of the medical profession have caused a huge amount of harm to patients, through ignorance and even disbelief.

Fighting to be diagnosed, to save relationships, to get (and keep) benefits, to find and try out treatments, to keep any kind of semblance of normality, is utterly exhausting and, on top of already having no energy to work with, often impossible. Relationships crumble. Friends disappear. Bills go unpaid. The chronically sick are the most likely group in society to be isolated, in debt, homeless or hopeless. We are extremely vulnerable. At the start, I lost my health, job, first marriage and home all within a few months.

In church, if you can even get there, you may find there is little understanding about what you need. People are keen to pray for you when you are sick, but if your miracle is not forthcoming within a couple of months, some people start to question your faith and even your desire to be healed. Some people have been kind, but I feel as if most have forgotten I exist since I have been unable to be physically present in any way. A few special souls remain in touch, but I know that if there were a rota for carrying me to the healing pool every day, it would be pretty hard to fill. Most of my interaction is now on social media, lots of it with fellow sufferers.

If you are coping with a chronic illness and/or a disability, then you are dealing daily with high levels of grief and disappointment. I mourn the opportunity to have children or a career, and my ability to do the things I love most in life, two of which are walking and reading. I can read, but only for a few minutes at a time, and when the illness was at its worst, not at all. For someone who used to read avidly for hours – for the whole day if I could get away with it – the fact that the world of books is virtually closed to me now is heartbreaking. And to go for a long walk on my own without a wheelchair and carer in the park or the woods, this is something I can hardly bear even to think of, let alone write about.

When you are long-term sick, you have no choice but to adapt. As with any loss, you find yourself dealing with complex emotions about the changes your life has gone through. In addition to coping with the physical limitations, symptoms, horrible exhaustion and pain, I regularly feel deeply angry, frustrated, broken and sometimes depressed. To start with I became an expert sulker and indulged in a lot of self-pity. I railed at God (occasionally I still do!), but thankfully his love is so all-encompassing that it only arouses his compassion.

To survive well you must reach a place of acceptance, whilst at the same time always being open to the possibility of healing. God has chosen to hold me, not heal me, but he embraces me very closely. You have to find new ways to thrive and learn patience, both with yourself and others, and perhaps especially your body, taking that loving forbearance to levels you never thought you could reach.

Because God is gracious, some enormous positives have also come out of my enforced stillness. God has used the time and seclusion to draw me into a deep prayer life, and to teach me how to listen for his still, small voice. He speaks into the silence even as he shares it with me, and is helping me to learn at his feet, to receive understandings, prayer pictures and seeings that constantly replenish my soul.

After a decade of this special time, he then surprised me by revealing that I had creative gifts I'd known little or nothing about. I have become a writer, poet and artist. I have to write in short bursts (this piece, for example, was written over a number of weeks) and to paint on a light drawing board on my lap, and none of it is less than exhausting. I don't believe God has caused me to suffer. But I do feel that given to him, God has used this illness to glorify himself through these things shared, and to bring me closer to his heart than I ever imagined possible.

In essence, what happens when you get chronically ill to this level is that your world shrinks. I spend more than twenty-two hours a day in one room, most of that in bed. Getting up, dressing, bathing, these are Herculean tasks, as is having a precious but short conversation with my husband, who cares for me beautifully. I would love to be healed of ME. But I take solace from the fact that with my daily given 'yes', the Lord has used my suffering and the smallness and isolation of my life to give me access to himself and his gifts in a way which, in a busy, well, noisy life, may not have come about. I relish that, and I treasure the bursts of creativity I can manage, and the grace of God that gets me through each day.

I hope in some little way to be glorifying him by painting his beautiful creation and writing about his faithfulness to me within this different life.

9

Surviving Abuse

The things that happened to me have shaped
me in so many ways. But they do not define me.
Abuse survivor[1]

Hearing a Voice from the Past

It is hard to find words to tell you my story, but I want to find
my voice.

I know I had left him, and that made it my fault in their
eyes. But it is by no means that simple. I seem to have spent my
life seeking sanctuary and never finding it, not once knowing
true shelter.

Four months it was, four months in my father's house before
he came to get me back. Months when I did not know whether
to hope for or fear his coming. Whether my life here, seeing my
disgrace mirrored in my father's eyes, was preferable to serving
my master: which place of powerlessness was best, or worst? In
either place I was just their possession, no rights, no control, no
say-so in my own future.

But come he did, and they played out their petty power games
under the guise of hospitality, both claiming me and neither

willing to let go. In the end my master won: he was the learned one, the one with influence. So off we set to an unknown future, my acquiescence the one thing I could decide to gift.

Him and his religion. His stubborn certainty that we were only safe with his people, as though every other group were tarnished and untrustworthy. So we carried on way past exhaustion, only to find ourselves marooned in some Godforsaken village until an apparent rescuer took us in. Again the men feasted and talked, ignoring me. But then came the voices, his door almost shattering under their assault, and the nightmare began.

I knew what they wanted, of course. Women always know. And I knew in my heart that the men would protect themselves, that I would eventually be thrown to the wolves baying at the door. Yet somehow I held on to a futile hope for rescue right up until the moment came.

He didn't look at me as he yanked me roughly to my feet, pulled me to the door. As he barely opened it, I scraped myself on its rough wood as I was expelled from the fragile safety of the house, sprawling in the dirt to face the angry faces from which all compassion had long been banished. I think something died inside me at that moment as the terror enveloped me.

I won't, can't, describe that night. I want to find a voice for my suffering, yes. But some things have too much horror to be given words. This is all I will say:

There are a thousand ways to end your life,
But none more terrible than this.
Each second an eternity as body and soul
Were stripped with vile disregard
As utterly alone my very humanity was trampled
Under the squalor of power and lust and dominance,
Sacrificed for his protection.

He slept the night while everything of meaning
Was ripped from my ravaged, bleeding soul.

I crawled back
Hoping against hope for sanctuary
But as my hand reached the door
I slipped away into dark recesses
Somewhere within and could not speak again.
And so he loaded me
Like goods to be bartered or delivered
And took me back – I cannot call it home.
There to complete the final degradation:
Hacked to pieces
Calling men to arms
As if violence could somehow make it right.
And as they fought to satisfy his injured pride
My honour was for ever sacrificed
And cries out still for restitution.

No one ever tells my story, even though my master's God put it
in his book. Yet the story, surely, needs to be told.

***

Judges 19 tells her story in this way:

In those days Israel had no king.
 Now a Levite who lived in a remote area in the hill country of
Ephraim took a concubine from Bethlehem in Judah. [2] But she was
unfaithful to him. She left him and went back to her parents' home
in Bethlehem, Judah. After she had been there for four months, [3] her
husband went to her to persuade her to return. He had with him his

servant and two donkeys. She took him into her parents' home, and when her father saw him, he gladly welcomed him. ⁴ His father-in-law, the woman's father, prevailed on him to stay; so he remained with him three days, eating and drinking, and sleeping there.

⁵ On the fourth day they got up early and he prepared to leave, but the woman's father said to his son-in-law, 'Refresh yourself with something to eat; then you can go.' ⁶ So the two of them sat down to eat and drink together. Afterwards the woman's father said, 'Please stay tonight and enjoy yourself.' ⁷ And when the man got up to go, his father-in-law persuaded him, so he stayed there that night. ⁸ On the morning of the fifth day, when he rose to go, the woman's father said, 'Refresh yourself. Wait till afternoon!' So the two of them ate together.

⁹ Then when the man, with his concubine and his servant, got up to leave, his father-in-law, the woman's father, said, 'Now look, it's almost evening. Spend the night here; the day is nearly over. Stay and enjoy yourself. Early tomorrow morning you can get up and be on your way home.' ¹⁰ But, unwilling to stay another night, the man left and went towards Jebus (that is, Jerusalem), with his two saddled donkeys and his concubine.

¹¹ When they were near Jebus and the day was almost gone, the servant said to his master, 'Come, let's stop at this city of the Jebusites and spend the night.'

¹² His master replied, 'No. We won't go into any city whose people are not Israelites. We will go on to Gibeah.' ¹³ He added, 'Come, let's try to reach Gibeah or Ramah and spend the night in one of those places.' ¹⁴ So they went on, and the sun set as they neared Gibeah in Benjamin. ¹⁵ There they stopped to spend the night. They went and sat in the city square, but no one took them in for the night.

¹⁶ That evening an old man from the hill country of Ephraim, who was living in Gibeah (the inhabitants of the place were Benjaminites), came in from his work in the fields. ¹⁷ When he

looked and saw the traveller in the city square, the old man asked, 'Where are you going? Where did you come from?'

¹⁸ He answered, 'We are on our way from Bethlehem in Judah to a remote area in the hill country of Ephraim where I live. I have been to Bethlehem in Judah and now I am going to the house of the LORD. No one has taken me in for the night. ¹⁹ We have both straw and fodder for our donkeys and bread and wine for ourselves your servants – me, the woman and the young man with us. We don't need anything.'

²⁰ 'You are welcome at my house,' the old man said. 'Let me supply whatever you need. Only don't spend the night in the square.' ²¹ So he took him into his house and fed his donkeys. After they had washed their feet, they had something to eat and drink.

²² While they were enjoying themselves, some of the wicked men of the city surrounded the house. Pounding on the door, they shouted to the old man who owned the house, 'Bring out the man who came to your house so we can have sex with him.'

²³ The owner of the house went outside and said to them, 'No, my friends, don't be so vile. Since this man is my guest, don't do this outrageous thing. ²⁴ Look, here is my virgin daughter, and his concubine. I will bring them out to you now, and you can use them and do to them whatever you wish. But as for this man, don't do such an outrageous thing.'

²⁵ But the men would not listen to him. So the man took his concubine and sent her outside to them, and they raped her and abused her throughout the night, and at dawn they let her go. ²⁶ At daybreak the woman went back to the house where her master was staying, fell down at the door and lay there until daylight.

²⁷ When her master got up in the morning and opened the door of the house and stepped out to continue on his way, there lay his concubine, fallen in the doorway of the house, with her hands on the threshold. ²⁸ He said to her, 'Get up; let's go.' But there was no answer. Then the man put her on his donkey and set out for home.

²⁹ When he reached home, he took a knife and cut up his concubine, limb by limb, into twelve parts and sent them into all the
areas of Israel. ³⁰ Everyone who saw it was saying to one another,
'Such a thing has never been seen or done, not since the day the
Israelites came up out of Egypt. Just imagine! We must do something! So speak up!'

This is a shocking story which I have never heard a sermon on
in decades of churchgoing. Or at least I hadn't until a friend of
mine, hearing I was writing this chapter, sent me a link to one
he had preached. Just the fact that he had done so moved me to
tears. This horrific story is so rarely dealt with that it seems this
woman has remained silent and unnamed not just in the story
but ever since, which is why I wanted to give her, and women
like her, a voice.

There is a sinister opening to the chapter – '*In those days
Israel had no king*' – hinting at a lack of societal structure the
impact of which the author makes even clearer in the closing
verse of Judges: '*In those days Israel had no king; everyone did
as they saw fit*'.[2] Kings held responsibility for ensuring people
knew and abided by the Torah, as well as to protect the weak
and vulnerable.

The story starts innocently enough with a Levite – also unnamed, but a teacher of the law and so an esteemed member of
that society. He has a concubine, essentially a kind of servant
wife who was a second-class member of the family but sometimes taken if, for example, a wife was infertile.[3] Her powerless
position is already in stark contrast with his.

It is not clear why she left: as the original text has been translated either as '*she was unfaithful*' or she '*became angry*' (e.g. NRSV),
which causes confusion as to who has been offended. Was she unwilling to be a second wife? For whatever reason she has returned

to her original home, and though it says that her master went to bring her back '*to speak to her heart*'[4] he does take four months to do so, which implies some motive other than affection and desperation to see her return. We are left wondering why, then? Was her work in the household missed? What was the attitude of her father to the return of his daughter, four months with her and then her husband's return?

When the Levite arrives at the father-in-law's home, the dynamic between the two men is very unclear. It reads as though there is initial cordiality between them, but their contact lessens as the days go by – demonstrated, for example, in them getting up together at first but later not doing so. Whatever the curious relationship between the men, eventually the master leaves with the concubine, whose lack of value is implied by the fact she is mentioned even after the donkeys.

He opts to go further than necessary in order to stay in a place of fellow-Israelites, ironically expecting to be safer there. However, no one took them in, despite the expectation in that culture of hospitality. An old man comes and recognises they are at risk if they stay outside. Something has gone badly wrong in this town that strangers are not safe in its square. Not just the nation, but this community has gone astray. At national, local and individual levels there is a complete lack of integrity and morality.

It transpires that even in this old man's house they are not safe. A gang arrive, demanding sex with the old man's male guest. To the reader at this point there are chilling parallels with Sodom and Gomorrah[5] – but they were pagan cities and these are Jews with clear moral laws. Both episodes are a dreadful travesty of hospitality, similar across cultures at that time. Yet even more terrible is that this host, who appeared at the start to be concerned for their safety, offers both his virgin daughter and the concubine of his guest to the mob instead.

They don't listen, but the man who supposedly had gone to 'speak to the concubine's heart' throws her out to the mob anyway to be subject to the most unspeakable violence and abuse in order to protect himself, instead of waiting or attempting to broker a solution. This violation continues throughout the night and is described with a telling brevity. Its naming is shocking enough.

In the morning, he sets out to go – apparently unconcerned about taking her too – and almost falls over her on the doorstep. There is a terrible poignancy as her hand is described as on the door, perhaps trying to crawl to a safety which was not going to be offered to her. All he does is tell her to get up – his first words to her throughout, and devoid of concern or compassion. When no answer comes from this traumatised woman, he doesn't even check if she is alive, and so we have no idea when she actually died.[6]

Whenever her death actually occurred, even then there is no dignity for her. Instead he seeks the wrong kind of retribution and so her body is dismembered and divided between the twelve tribes as a call to more violence. It was not unusual in those times to call others to arms with pieces of an animal,[7] but to do so with a powerless woman, sacrificed for his own safety, is an act of unspeakable brutality. It seems only fitting that there is no mention of God in this bleak story, which continues with catastrophic violence in battle. The next stories after the end of Judges are a curious contrast:[8] God's compassionate treatment of Hannah in 1 Samuel in the Hebrew Bible and the story of Ruth in the Greek Bible. Both the Hebrew original and the Greek translation have the same books, but in slightly different order. However, these more gentle narratives cannot remove the horror of this shocking and terrifying story.

***

Sadly, abuse is as much an issue in our day. Here one woman finds her voice:

Hearing a Voice from the Present

I was 6 when it started. Just 6. A little girl. Up to then life had been fairly mundane. I lived with my parents and two younger brothers in a household which from the outside was unremarkable. But then the song of my life, just beginning, became discordant. The ship tilted, and it has never found equilibrium from that day.

I was so, so confused at the change which, step by step, insidiously came over bedtime . . . those times I had enjoyed with stories and a cuddle which had made me feel so very loved and safe. One day it was different – just a small change, but it was the start of things slowly not being like they were before. The times I had so enjoyed became times that made me at first confused and unsure, but as things continued, upset and afraid. What had I done wrong? I must have done something wrong. But what, and how could I put it right? Perhaps if I was just very quiet, tried to be a good girl, I could make it better, whatever it was that I had done. I've been saying sorry with my whole life ever since.

It is painful to describe, even years on, the horror of those times. Once I got to bed, which I put off as long as possible, daytime clothes being somehow a protection, I used to make myself as small as I could, curling in a ball under the blanket when I heard his footsteps on the stairs. I tried holding my breath as though that might make me disappear. But nothing stopped it happening. I felt utterly powerless, so small and defenceless. It is not that he was violent. He simply said that was how I needed to love Daddy because Daddy loved and needed me so very much. And I did love him. But I didn't love what was happening, which made me feel sad and muddled and dirty, and a very, very bad person.

I tried to escape. Not physically, of course. He was so big and I was so little. But I tried to go somewhere inside so that I was there but not there, an unhelpful and lasting divide of body and soul which seemed the only way to manage something which I was totally unable to find a way to make sense of.

At school I created a fantasy life. I told my friends stories about family times and holidays which were complete fiction. When a little older, I started to write stories – a parallel world where I could take refuge, creating characters who could be safe people in my life. I dreamed about being rescued. To this day I am unbelievably – almost unbearably – moved by films where at the end someone is freed and held. I longed for that security and protection which I had once known and which had so inexplicably been taken away.

I tried, just once, to tell my mother. Unsure what to say, not having any words to describe what was happening, I asked her if she would put me to bed. She didn't even look at me. 'Those are your and Daddy's special times,' she said. I've never known if she was aware – but how could she be and let it continue? I have so many unanswered questions.

I started to sleepwalk, waking only when I sat down on the cold surface of my dressing table. That was frightening in its own way, but less so than the nightmares, nightly scenes of terror which still happen today. Yet nobody outside of the house noticed anything, as far as I could tell, even when one day, to my mother's fury, I said at a friend's house that I didn't want to go home. In one way I didn't want anyone to know; yet in another, I did. So I became expert at concealing the internal chaos under a calm and even smiling exterior. It was – and still is – both a useful skill and a terrible, isolating trap.

And then, when I was 10, my father became ill. Initially I felt relief as he was confined to bed and then hospital. No more night-time visits. Within six months he had died. But then the guilt and shame overwhelmed me. I was sure it was my fault. I hadn't loved him well enough. Somehow my internal muddle and mess had made him ill. I carried that sense of responsibility for decades. Maybe I still do. I felt as though the torment ought to be finally at an end, whereas in reality it was just beginning. It was a terrible legacy to leave the child he said he loved.

I grew up, left home, and somehow crawled my way to adulthood. My mother died when I was in my late teens, so my quasi-independent persona served me well. I even came to faith, though unsurprisingly I related more to Jesus than to God as Father. Some aspects of faith I found difficult, in particular in charismatic churches where there was so much language of intimacy. I received prayer at times for 'inner heal- ing', still without revealing too much, but wrestled with the idea of Jesus being with us through our painful past as to me that made him some kind of divine voyeur who watched but did nothing. At times I felt angry in worship, at other times experiencing a desperate longing to really connect with God co-existing uneasily with a fear of him coming too close.

The façade I had built for years held up well. Underneath, though, the story was very different. I was constantly in pain, wrestling with a sense of self-hatred that clung to me despite a blossoming career and friendships which, although I never told anyone the truth, served to assuage a little of the inner loneliness. I sought to swallow my emotions, literally, in order to hold them at bay, but no liquid anaesthetic lasted long and the pain returned. I abandoned that way of coping, shored up my defences, and carried on the daily battle to look normal.

Inevitably, it caught up with me in the end. I began to lose the capacity to hold the mask together and reluctantly sought help. It was life-saving, and I am very grateful, though at times I thought I would never make it. And indeed doubted that I wanted to. There has been a long path to walk since, and I know I am not as I once was, even though complete healing has so far evaded me. However much it would shock almost everyone who knows me, I know there is a broken little girl inside who still needs loving but who never gets held or heard.

In all that time one of the most helpful realisations was that, before the crucifixion, Jesus himself found himself powerless and at the mercy of the soldiers, abused and broken. To understand that he gets it, really understands, has been something I have tried to hold on to in the dark times. Once, not long ago, I was in a meeting where we were encouraged to think of our lives as a melody God was singing over us. I was distraught. All I could think was that my life was a lament. Then, a quiet voice within: 'If you will let me sing it with you, it will become beautiful.'

My hope is that somehow it will.

10

Confronting Death

> *I am the resurrection and the life. The one who*
> *believes in me will live, even though they die;*
> *and whoever lives by believing in me will never*
> *die. Do you believe this?*[1]

Jesus

Hearing a Voice from the Past

I am in hell. This dying is hell. I can't think of anything worse.
I don't want to die, but I don't want to live much longer like
this either.

Looking back, I am struggling to work out how it came to
this. Perhaps there is no point in asking, 'Why?' I made some
choices along the way – bad decisions, which resulted in this
bloody end. But I am asking the question anyway, futile as it is.

As I labour for every breath, I am at the mercy of memories which crowd in on me, unwanted intruders invading my
oxygen-starved mind. Like a waking nightmare I toss and turn
mentally in my immobile body. I remember the small boy I
once was, playing in the dusty street, a bundle of potential,
laughing with my friends. I recall the teenage years, struggling

to find who I was and where I belonged. The growing resentment at the struggle just to have enough to live on, while others flaunted their wealth, wearing it like a badge of honour even if it was inherited or gained by cheating the rest of us. Bitterness grew in me, festering in my spirit until I decided that honesty profited nothing, and started me on the road which has brought me here, at the mercy of callous soldiers and curious bystanders. My family are ashamed of me, but not as much as I am of myself. The humiliation of being strung up here naked is nothing to what I feel inside, the heat of my shame washing over me more powerfully even than this oppressive heat.

So enveloped in my own thoughts, it has taken me some time to think about those others being crucified with me. Those damn Romans love to line the roads with us, a deterrent to any fool who might try insurrection. Though I could hardly ignore the words of the man next to me as they strung him up. Praying forgiveness for these brutes to his God who surely has forsaken him? That makes no sense to me. The man on the other side, him I can understand, spitting venom at the soldiers, pain expressed in anger. When he turned on the man between us, initially I joined in too. Less vocally, but muttering under my breath at this mug offering forgiveness that no one wanted or deserved.

I never thought I would end my life at the hands of these foreign invaders. But then I never really thought about the end of my life at all. Who does, until there is no option?

But as the interminable minutes stretched on, I became curious. There was something different about him, something I could sense even from my sidelong glances. A quiet dignity which somehow came through even though presumably his pain was no less than mine. Then there were the women, standing there with tear-lined faces, their grief palpable but their love equally so. Who was he, to inspire such devotion?

There was something more than that, though. I began to fear I was losing my mind, because I felt as though the whole world – the cosmos, even – was somehow watching, waiting, holding its breath for . . . for what? How could this man's death possibly matter beyond a few family and friends? Yet that curiosity kept nudging me, like a starving dog worrying at my heels. So from my parched throat I managed to gasp out words directed at a passer-by. 'What's he here for?' They stopped to look. 'It says King of the Jews.'

'King of the Jews'? What does that mean? Just some other rabble-rouser, seeking a gang of discontents in a futile attempt to overthrow the weight of the Roman Empire? There had been plenty of those . . . but they always exuded an anger, a fury that seemed entirely lacking in this man. I struggled to turn my head and look, and caught his eye: he had turned to me as though he had sensed what I was doing. I could hear the man the other side of him, still furiously blaspheming at this stranger who inexplicably seemed to be enraging him even more than the soldiers who had nailed him there. I continued to hold the man's gaze. Such understanding was there, such gentleness, as though he could see into my very soul, knowing every wrong choice, each stupid act of rebellion against a God I was not at that moment sure if I believed in, and yet gently holding it all like a parent holding a child whose foolishness has caused both of them pain. The one clear thing amid my disintegrating world was this – this man was innocent. And perhaps even more. So with diminishing strength I called across to the man on the other side of him: '*Don't you fear God, since you are under the same sentence? We are punished justly, for we are getting what our deeds deserve. But this man has done nothing wrong.*'

I'm still not sure what any of this means. I don't know for sure the identity of this stranger who fate – or the God he clearly believes in – has put me beside for my dying hours. Yet I sense something in him – yes, even something regal. Something powerful even amid his utter helplessness, hung like me on a cross. So I am going to take one last desperate gamble, staking my future on this man.

As I gasp for breath, yes, I am afraid of what is ahead. Not so much death, as the dying.

Lord, will you remember me when you come into your kingdom?

***

His story is from Luke 23:32–43:

[32] Two other men, both criminals, were also led out with him to be executed. [33] When they came to the place called the Skull, they crucified him there, along with the criminals – one on his right, the other on his left. [34] Jesus said, 'Father, forgive them, for they do not know what they are doing.' And they divided up his clothes by casting lots.

[35] The people stood watching, and the rulers even sneered at him. They said, 'He saved others; let him save himself if he is God's Messiah, the Chosen One.'

[36] The soldiers also came up and mocked him. They offered him wine vinegar [37] and said, 'If you are the king of the Jews, save yourself.'

[38] There was a written notice above him, which read: THIS IS THE KING OF THE JEWS.

[39] One of the criminals who hung there hurled insults at him: 'Aren't you the Messiah? Save yourself and us!'

[40] But the other criminal rebuked him. 'Don't you fear God,' he said, 'since you are under the same sentence? [41] We are punished

justly, for we are getting what our deeds deserve. But this man has done nothing wrong.'

[42] Then he said, 'Jesus, remember me when you come into your kingdom.'

[43] Jesus answered him, 'Truly I tell you, today you will be with me in paradise.'

It is always challenging to write anything about the crucifixion. Somehow it feels like treading on holy ground. Depictions of the crucifixion (notably the film *The Passion of the Christ*) have centred on the physical aspects of the suffering, which were admittedly extreme. Even before the actual crucifixion, most victims had been flogged, causing multiple lacerations which carrying the harsh wood of the crossbeam to the site of the crucifixion would have exacerbated. Once at the place chosen for the execution, nails were driven through the wrists, causing excruciating nerve pain and often dislocating the shoulders. Being hung in this way makes breathing impossible, so those being tortured would try to raise themselves up, despite suffering muscle cramps and shock from the beatings. This allowed them to briefly catch a fuller breath. It is likely that the seven phrases[2] Jesus spoke from the cross were those he was able to speak in brief interludes of gasping for air. In the end, though (if necessary hastened by their legs being broken to prevent changing position to alleviate the gradual asphyxiation[3]), the person would usually die from suffocation[4] as the weight of their body pulled down on the diaphragm.

However, crucifixion was not just intended to be physically brutal. It was a particularly barbaric form of crime prevention, with the misdemeanour of the crucified being displayed as a deterrent to anyone contemplating the same offence. Crucifixions were public, and those dying in this way were usually stripped naked. They were intended to be demeaning. We can assume that placing Jesus between two thieves[5] was deliberate: a ploy to further humiliate what his accusers would have seen as a self-styled holy man.

Families had to watch loved-ones suffer for hours – sometimes even days – and then often the bodies were left there as a continued reminder of their wrongdoing, vulnerable to all kinds of other indignities, with relatives deprived of the opportunity to honour those they loved with a respectful committal. The mental cruelty was extreme and some of those being crucified broke down mentally long before death.

There are various legends surrounding the particular two companions to Jesus in his final hours, but they are just that – legends. We know nothing of them. What was it that caused one man to rail against Jesus, and the other to see something in him that made him ask this one last desperate request? Had he encountered Jesus before? Or heard of him? We have so many unanswered questions.

In Jesus' answer – '*today you will be with me in paradise*' – the word translated in English as 'paradise' is interesting. It is of Persian origin meaning a walled garden. If a Persian king wanted to honour someone, he invited them to walk in the palace garden with him. This puts a slightly different slant on what the dying man is being offered. Not just a place in heaven, a promise of life beyond death, but an honoured position, as a companion to the King of all creation.

It is sometimes said that there are four biblical gardens: firstly, the garden of Eden, signifying humanity's downfall as a result of our desire for the control which is rightfully God's; secondly, the garden of Gethsemane where Jesus literally sweats it out and the future of the cosmos hangs by a thread; thirdly, the garden at the place of Jesus' crucifixion and burial[6] and fourthly, the garden of Revelation 2:7 (and Revelation 22) where life is fully restored when God finally makes all things right. This passage reveals to us a fifth garden – where the God of mercy invites all his flawed and broken children to walk with him in a place of privilege. Humiliation and shame are transformed into respect and dignity for those seeking Jesus – for whatever reason and at whatever stage of life. It is never too late, as this nameless man discovered.

***

Confronting death, however, is never easy . . .

Hearing a Voice from the Present

There are so many things which are painful in my current life – if I can call it life. Physically, but also emotionally. As I look back, it is almost impossible to believe that this is happening to me. Yet in other ways it is far too real.

Some eighteen months ago, I had what seemed at the time like a simple fall, which injured my back. Back pain – the common cold of every NHS physiotherapy department. A nuisance, yes, but I thought no more of it. Looking back, I realise that it was possibly not the fall that caused the problem with my back, but a creeping, insidious weakness in my back which had caused the fall. But 20/20 vision is always the gift of hindsight and never a current reality. Ironically, I had seen a neurologist some months before, but they too had not realised what was happening.

So it seemed at the time this was just a minor inconvenience as I waited for the next stage of my life. There were so many plans: dreams of a new home in the West Country where my partner and I could be nearer to the nature we love so much: both to enjoy it and to contribute in some way, volunteering time and skills. It is so easy to take life and vitality for granted and so devastatingly heartbreaking when they are snatched away.

When things did not improve, despite my systematic exercising, more tests followed, and in time came the shattering diagnosis. Motor neurone disease. By then I had an inkling, but the hammer blow was no less for that: somehow it still came as a shock. Suddenly the years I thought I had stretching ahead had diminished to – what? No one could be sure. Statistics – yes, I can quote those. A third of people die within a year and more than half within two years of diagnosis.[7] And no, it doesn't help for you to quote me Stephen Hawking's fifty-five years. Please don't.

At first, I thought I had achieved a kind of stoic quasi-acceptance. I compiled a bucket list, places I wanted to visit, and began to work through them. Although a wheelchair was at first beckoning and then, more swiftly than I had hoped, necessary, I could still do some of the things I enjoyed. Even at these early stages, though, it became apparent that the road ahead consisted of one demoralising loss after another. My beloved camera became too heavy to hold, and then even a paintbrush, and I grieved the life of creative expression I had enjoyed. Some places became inaccessible, my world shrinking after a lifetime of travel. I could no longer simply decide to do something spontaneous. Still, there were fleeting moments of pleasure. Amid the bewildering array of feelings, appointments and questions, my partner and I decided to get married, and distracted ourselves with wedding plans. It had never occurred to me that I would go down the aisle in a wheelchair, but friends and the church family I had recently found rallied around to make it a special day.

However, just before the wedding, a step-change occurred. My breathing began to be affected. MND impacts different parts of the body, depending on the particular neurones that are involved, and I had not bargained on my breathing being affected this soon after diagnosis. A visit to the respiratory department resulted in another piece of shocking news. Without a ventilator I probably only had weeks to live. With it, perhaps months. So began my symbiotic relationship with my portable ventilator, which compensates for my weakened breathing muscles by forcing in extra air. I can take the mask off (ever-increasingly briefly) to talk or eat, but it has become indispensable, travelling with me wherever I go. A companion unsought and unwelcomed yet needed.

Not being able to breathe is terrifying. I suppose it is because it is such a fundamental part of our urge to live. A newborn gasps automatically for a breath as soon as they are delivered – it is a basic instinct and when for some reason we cannot breathe, or breathe easily, fear is our immediate and overwhelming response. I am afraid of developing an infection which further diminishes my breathing. I am afraid, too, of becoming helpless and at the mercy of others, unable to do anything for myself. I suffer bouts of panic almost as debilitating as the illness, and as medications which might help with the anxiety can exacerbate other symptoms, so far nothing has been helpful. Looking ahead to my increasing weakness and helplessness, I am unsure how I will cope. In a way, when I become bedridden it will be a relief, because movement such as transfers from bed to wheelchair or chair to toilet are so uncomfortable and exhausting and make me even more breathless. Yet when I am merely a body in a bed, what will there be to live for?

There is a horrible vicious circle. The use of the ventilator has traumatised my nostrils, which means my nose gets blocked, and a huge proportion of my waking thoughts are on how to keep them clear, or unblock them, so that I can breathe. My hearing is affected, too, by excess mucus. Crying – which I want to do a lot – makes it worse and so I try not to cry, even though there is so much to grieve. Old age is a succession of losses – independence, mobility, friends, activities, and control over one's body – but whereas these usually come gradually over time, I have been catapulted prematurely into a phase of life I was not in any way ready for. My body is changing in ways I do not like and cannot control – it is not the body I knew all my life. We are such a mix of memories and plans for the future, and I have only the former, which bring me pain as I remember places I can never revisit and things which brought me joy of which I feel I have been robbed.

I have a faith, and in the early days I sought to draw on it and find support through it. At the start, coming back to church after some years, I felt as though God was speaking to me, reassuring me that he was travelling with me. As time has progressed, though, I have found it more difficult to sense God's presence. At times I literally cry out for help. I feel as though God has gone, deserted me. He has not answered my prayers – I don't mean for healing, but for the smaller things which would make a difference. Yet I do appreciate people praying with me, and for me. At this point I am not sure how the rest of the journey will affect my fragile sense of relationship with God. In some ways it is good to be in an atmosphere of worship, when I have the energy – despite wheelchair and ventilator, at times I can manage to be at church – but in other ways frustrating. I am aware of the noise of the ventilator and cannot always hear what is happening. Somewhere amid this spiritual searching is the need to make sense of my life. What was it for? How will I be remembered? What enables any of us to find purpose? How, in these final months, able to do so little, can I find value? Is it really in simply being a beloved child of the creator – can I believe and hang on to that? And the biggest question – is this all there is, or is there life after death? Will I know the free and full life, released from my current body with all its restrictions, which my faith promises?

I am afraid of so many things. But I know my faith has been real. I remember renewing my baptismal vows in the River Jordan. I appreciate those who pray for me. And the Jesus who I said those vows to said he is 'the resurrection and the life'.

11

Finding Hope

*Praise be to the God and Father of our Lord Jesus
Christ! In his great mercy he has given us new
birth into a living hope through the resurrection
of Jesus Christ from the dead . . .*[1]

Peter, apostle of Jesus

Hearing a Voice from the Past

There is nothing more painful than losing somebody you love.

I'm not sure I can even begin to tell you how terrible it was.
Jesus – my friend, the one Cleopas and I had grown to admire,
to follow, to love. The one from who life and vitality, somehow
quite unlike mere human joy and vigour, simply oozed from
every pore. The one whose eyes danced with laughter and filled
with tears of compassion. The one who, we had thought, could
be all that we had hoped for.

Not any more. That had all gone, snatched from us. I had to
go, of course, to see him die. I couldn't let my fear and squeam-
ishness lead to me deserting him when he needed me most,
and so the other women and I gathered at the terrible scene.
His mother and aunt were there – I could not imagine how

their hearts must have been ripped out by the sight of him, so vulnerable and exposed to every taunt. It seemed as though the world as we knew it was ending. That Godforsaken darkness, making me feel as if every hint of life had been sucked out of the universe. And oh! That terrible, terrible cry of utter desolation as, with breath wrung from his weakening lungs, he screamed out: '*Eloi, Eloi, lema sabachthani?*'[2] I felt in that moment that God had abandoned us too. We clung to each other as though our physical closeness could ward off the horror, and tried unsuccessfully to hold Mary upright.

But now it was over, and on the third day there was nothing for it but to head home and try to work out how to put our shattered lives back together with him gone. Our pain threatened to tip over into anger, as it often can, not helped by our having slightly different opinions about the report of the empty tomb. We were throwing ideas backwards and forwards between us about it all. Part of me didn't want to go back home until we could find out what had happened, but Cleopas was protective and thought we would be safer back in Emmaus. The communal pain of us all together was becoming overwhelming. Besides, what was the point of waiting? It was finished.

When the stranger drew alongside us, instinctively we stopped for a moment as he asked what we were discussing. I was irritated but held my tongue. Once the decision was made to leave, I just wanted to get back to our village and we still had a couple of hours walking ahead. I longed to reach the sanctuary of home, try to find comfort in the everyday things which never changed: lighting a fire, fetching water, preparing a meal – small signs that some things, however trivial and meaningless now, would go on. None of us can see straight when we are in pain and we need something simple and familiar to hold on to.

I was quietly incredulous when our companion seemed not to know about Jesus. You didn't need to be his follower to know all about what happened. Cleopas was remarkably patient, I thought, explaining. So imagine my shock when he called us foolish and slow to believe! If we weren't together walking the same direction on the road, I might have been a lot more forthright, but something about him caught my attention. He started to explain that the Messiah had to suffer, it was part of God's plan, and as he took us through those scriptures which we knew so well, it was as if they had been given new life and I saw them with fresh eyes. I was intrigued and wanted to know more, and so, of course, as we arrived home we invited him in. We were both desperate to hear all that he had to say.

So I did all those familiar things – lit the fire, fetched the water, prepared a meal. Somehow now, though, they were not just to stave off the chasm of despair. He watched me carefully, and then as I placed it on the table, to my surprise, as if *he* were hosting *us*, not the other way round, he took the bread, gave thanks and broke it. In an instant I suddenly realised – it was Jesus! Cleopas and I turned to each other, recognition dawning on us both simultaneously, and we shrieked in delight, only to find that he had disappeared. I'm not young, but we danced with delight, and clung together in joyous celebration, so differently from the way the women had held each other at the cross.

He's alive! He's alive! We need to share the news!

***

Luke 24:13–35 tells the story this way:

¹³ Now that same day two of them were going to a village called Emmaus, about seven miles from Jerusalem. ¹⁴ They were talking

with each other about everything that had happened. ¹⁵ As they talked and discussed these things with each other, Jesus himself came up and walked along with them; ¹⁶ but they were kept from recognising him.

¹⁷ He asked them, 'What are you discussing together as you walk along?'

They stood still, their faces downcast. ¹⁸ One of them, named Cleopas, asked him, 'Are you the only one visiting Jerusalem who does not know the things that have happened there in these days?'

¹⁹ 'What things?' he asked.

'About Jesus of Nazareth,' they replied. 'He was a prophet, powerful in word and deed before God and all the people. ²⁰ The chief priests and our rulers handed him over to be sentenced to death, and they crucified him; ²¹ but we had hoped that he was the one who was going to redeem Israel. And what is more, it is the third day since all this took place. ²² In addition, some of our women amazed us. They went to the tomb early this morning ²³ but didn't find his body. They came and told us that they had seen a vision of angels, who said he was alive. ²⁴ Then some of our companions went to the tomb and found it just as the women had said, but they did not see Jesus.'

²⁵ He said to them, 'How foolish you are, and how slow to believe all that the prophets have spoken! ²⁶ Did not the Messiah have to suffer these things and then enter his glory?' ²⁷ And beginning with Moses and all the Prophets, he explained to them what was said in all the Scriptures concerning himself.

²⁸ As they approached the village to which they were going, Jesus continued on as if he were going further. ²⁹ But they urged him strongly, 'Stay with us, for it is nearly evening; the day is almost over.' So he went in to stay with them.

³⁰ When he was at the table with them, he took bread, gave thanks, broke it and began to give it to them. ³¹ Then their eyes

were opened and they recognised him, and he disappeared from their sight. [32] They asked each other, 'Were not our hearts burning within us while he talked with us on the road and opened the Scriptures to us?'

[33] They got up and returned at once to Jerusalem. There they found the Eleven and those with them, assembled together [34] and saying, 'It is true! The Lord has risen and has appeared to Simon.' [35] Then the two told what had happened on the way, and how Jesus was recognised by them when he broke the bread.

For many people, this rates as one of the most beautiful of all the Bible stories. It is a rich story, which works both as a straightforward account of the encounter of two people with Jesus, and as one with many deeper meanings illustrating the way we too can encounter Jesus even in the midst of loss and distress.

It is possible that the two people were husband and wife[3] and, if so, it would make sense that they were travelling home from Jerusalem together, trying to process things by talking them through. The word used of their conversation actually suggests strong debate – perhaps, as well as asking each other in anguish why Jesus had to die, they are disputing the accounts of the empty tomb which they report to Jesus later and which would have already started to circulate in the wider circle of disciples, as this was now Sunday afternoon/evening. As is equally true for many people today, just hearing that others reported the tomb was empty was not enough for them to believe that Jesus was alive. Actually this and other stories indicating the disciples' incredulity and scepticism add weight to the veracity of Jesus' resurrection – the early church would not have invented stories of that kind which might diminish the early heroes of the faith.

It is clear as the story unfolds that the two travellers are in despair. A stranger comes alongside them whose intrusion they could have resented or who could easily have been a spy (the disciples are in hiding at this point[4]), yet either from courage or despair they pour out the sadness of their hearts, admitting to having been his followers and to have hoped (past tense) that he was the Messiah. Now, though, all their expectations lie in ruins. They are bereaved and traumatised by everything they have experienced. It can be easy for us, because we know how the story ends, to underestimate the desolation they felt. It was absolute.

All the disciples had lost everything at the crucifixion. At the simplest and most poignant level, they had lost their best friend. They had listened to him, and he to them. They had eaten and laughed together. They had trusted him with their lives. But they had lost so much more even than that. In believing him to be the Messiah, they had expected him to defeat Israel's enemies and free them from tyranny, setting everything right, as God intended. Now those same oppressors had crucified him – not just destroying his life, but doing so in the most painful and humiliating way: strung up and ridiculed like a criminal. This made no sense if he was Israel's liberator, and so all their hopes and dreams had been crushed too. A suffering Messiah was not in anyone's thinking, despite the scriptures which we assume were among those Jesus shared with them.[5] As far as they are concerned, it is over, and they feel abandoned and bereft. Their hopes are as dead as their friend and have been buried with him.

It is noticeable that in a number of resurrection stories even his closest followers do not recognise Jesus.[6] It is possible to speculate on logical reasons why this is – in this instance, for example, the two travellers are not expecting to see him and in their distress, travelling into the setting sun,[7] may not have really looked. The language '*kept from recognising him*' also raises the possibility that Jesus wanted to have this conversation with them before they knew who he was. However, it does seem that Jesus' resurrected body was both (at times) recognisable and also different. We need to allow for mystery here.

Jesus asks them a question he, of course, knows the answers to: '*What are you discussing together as you walk along?*' Even when Cleopas expresses astonishment that this stranger doesn't know, Jesus encourages him to tell the story. This is so essential for bereaved people, to be able to voice what has happened to them and everything they feel. Telling stories is powerful and potentially healing. Jesus was much better at asking questions and then listening than we often are.

Once that has happened, Jesus embarks on some teaching which Luke (rather frustratingly!) summarises in a single sentence: '*And beginning with Moses and all the Prophets, he explained to them what was said in all the Scriptures concerning himself.*' The aim is clearly to show that his suffering, far from obliterating God's plan, as they feared, was actually central to it. Together with their later realisation of the way their hearts 'burned' listening to Jesus' words, it serves as a reminder that good Bible study can bring head and heart together in a unique way. As such it is also a salutary reminder of the huge importance of the task to all those, in whatever context, who are responsible for teaching the Bible to others.[8]

What they are hearing intrigues them, and so when they reach their home they invite him in, despite Jesus, who never forces himself on anyone, being apparently about to travel on. Presumably this is more than just the cultural expectation of hospitality, but a genuine fascination with what he is saying. At the meal, offering food being customary for guests, Jesus takes the bread, gives thanks and breaks it and, in an echo of the eating of the fruit in Genesis,[9] their eyes are opened. This time, however, it is in a very different way to the disaster of Genesis, being instead a life-giving moment of revelation of his identity. From a first 'meal' which symbolised so much destruction, here in contrast is the first one after the final defeat of sin and death. Just as realisation strikes, Jesus disappears from their sight. They understand the significance of how they felt on the road, and despite the late hour they are too excited to wait, instead heading back to Jerusalem to share the extraordinary news with Jesus' inner circle of disciples, who have joyful news of their own to share.

It is interesting that they recognised Jesus when he broke bread. This couple would not have been present at the Last Supper, but presumably there would have been other occasions when they saw Jesus break bread, so was it something in the familiarity of the way he did that? Barbara Brown Taylor writes movingly, in a talk on a later section of this same chapter in Luke, about how our hands tell their own story and how we can recognise each other from them.[10] Did they see nail marks? Whatever the significance in the original context of their recognition of Jesus in the breaking of the bread, it is a reminder that people of every age and across every era, language and culture have and do encounter Jesus as the bread is broken in communion services. Equally, it is a powerful image of the way in which God can meet us in the very ordinary moments of our day and transform them.

One of the most wonderful aspects of this story, aside from the exhilarating historical truth of the resurrection it portrays, is what it signifies. Here Jesus walks with them at the most desperate moment of their lives. He is hidden, but he is not absent.[11] This is a stunning truth. There are many times, at least for most of us, when God feels absent, and painfully this is most often true when we go through difficult seasons. This story is a reminder that Jesus walks with us then too, even when we cannot feel it, and can somehow help us to make sense of things. A great deal of the time, that happens when we walk alongside each other, as the apostle Paul points out: '*Praise be to the God and Father of our Lord Jesus Christ, the Father of compassion and the God of all comfort, who comforts us in all our troubles, so that we can comfort those in any trouble with the comfort we ourselves receive from God.*'[12]

There is hope, even in the face of death.

***

Hearing a Voice from the Present

Loss. It is so very, very hard.

From an early age I wanted either to drive a steam engine or operate a bacon slicer at Sainsbury's, but having become a Christian I decided to teach children RE. After university I took a teaching post and it was in this role that I first met the young man who was to become my stepson. In my teaching role I was linked with an organisation that involved me in helping to run a Christian Union at a school. One thing we did was to bring the lads down to Southend to see the lights. The young man was a boarder at the school as his mum had died, and he came on the coach with the rest. Later I met his dad – fifty years on and you're hearing the story – it was a triumph of church matchmaking! We were married about a year later.

When he came to the end of his schooling my stepson, who had muscular dystrophy, opted not to come home to us but to move into a home/hostel. Our relationship always continued to be special, though, and I was 'Mum' to him whereas his older brother has always called me by my Christian name.

My husband and I had a daughter and, despite his disability, she and my stepson were devoted to each other – as a toddler she abandoned her buggy and rode instead on the back of his scooter. We had to watch him deteriorate, which was so hard, but we were surrounded by family, friends and church family, which was a huge comfort.

He gradually became weaker, and we were called to come to see him and spend the day just being with him. It had been arranged for us to spend the night with a Christian couple living nearby. In the morning we were told – though not before we had been given a lovely breakfast – that he had died in his sleep during the night. We went to his room to see him at peace and I shall never forget my husband's cry of anguish: 'My son, my son.' I still find it difficult to read the Bible story where David's heart is broken for the death of his son Absalom.[13]

We struggled with the incredible pain of losing him. I still do sometimes. What somehow sustained us in those terrible days was the hope that death is not the end and we will all meet again. My last words to him were: 'See you in the morning.' I never realised at the time that it would be a very long wait.

We had given up asking 'Why?' years before he died and sought instead to hold on to God's faithfulness. Our family hymn is 'Great is Thy Faithfulness'. As a teenager I had been suddenly paralysed and expected to die, but to the doctors' amazement I recovered when I became a Christian – why was I healed and not him? A dear friend who died of cancer a few years ago responded to the question 'Why?' with 'Why not?'. But I do know that the practical support we had – like the breakfast that terrible day – made such a difference.

At the time of his funeral it was crucial for us to share our pain and loss with others. Physical touch at times like this is so important and we needed the hugs which others gave us. We had to take one day at a time – sometimes an hour or even a minute at a time – and we were upheld by God's promise that '*as your days, so shall your strength be*'[14] and by Isaiah 40, especially verse 31: '*those who hope in the* LORD *will renew their strength. They will soar on wings like eagles, they will run and not grow weary, they will walk and not be faint.*' Immediately after his death, everything felt numb and all we could do was just cling to each other. Telling our daughter was indescribably hard – she reacted by screaming in a way I'd never heard her do before or since, whereas my other stepson went into his shell.

Amid all the practical arrangements that needed organising, we were still numb and could not register much. The funeral service was led by a minister who had a son with a different type of muscular dystrophy. The main imprint the funeral left me with was that a person's life is not measured by the length of days, and that he had led a full life in spite of his disability. Many tears were shed, yet at times a phrase or a joke or a gesture would trigger memories which interwove the joyful with the sad. These and various words from the Bible helped us to keep confidence in our God who gave us Jesus.

One way to continue to love and remember him was fundraising for research and support for those suffering from muscular dystrophy, though the main grief therapy was washing up mugs galore in the staff-room kitchen. I found I needed to be with others rather than shutting myself away – not that I had any option, as I was still teaching at the time.

This was some years ago now, so a lot has melted into the past. However, even today, I still react to a wheelchair and give thanks that so much by way of mobility help has improved over the years. I don't think many wheelchair users still travel in guards' vans on the trains and share their mugs of tea! One guard even came to our home and gave my stepson some budgies so he could breed them and have an aviary. Such kindness was an expression of the kindness of God which we experienced in so many ways.

We continue to talk about him because he is still part of our family, but his loss was not to be the only devastating one. The next was my husband. How can I describe him? Only one word – irreplaceable! He was a real character – he was a church secretary for many years and in the days when church secretaries gave the notices before the service started, folk would be waiting for his 'funny' of the week. Over the years there were never two the same. Without him half of me, in many ways, has gone and that was true from the day he died.

We knew that he was ill. On the day before he went into hospital, I was woken up in the night and heard a voice clearly saying to me, 'He's not yours, let him go.' I've never experienced anything like it before or since. He died three days later. The morning after that dream I also got a letter from a very precious friend who did not live locally expressing his sorrow at my loss and sharing all that he loved about him . . . Our friend was able later to share in the funeral service. I believe that God gave me those two experiences to help me through those terrible days.

My husband's family are undertakers, although his side of the family are no longer involved, and so we obviously used that firm. I taught two of the three brothers who are in the business and one of them drove us to the church. It was he who helped me out of the car and escorted me in. That simple thing is such a lovely memory, as is so many of our church family gathering to prepare the wake after the ceremony and the fact that we could all pray together before the other events of the day.

In those early days I struggled to see couples holding hands, especially in church, and if I'm honest, I was jealous of them. Now I can accept it more and can rejoice at their happiness with each other. Touch means so much and that was what I missed and still do – my bed is so empty. There is no arm put over me to say goodnight; no snoring either! From those early days (and still today) I'd get really angry when people moaned about their husbands without any valid reason, and I have been known to reprimand some friends . . . You find a way to go on but it is still so very painful, such an ache, at times.

The Psalms – so ruthlessly honest – were my journey companions in those early days and expressed my inner yearnings so often. Psalm 46:10 urged me to '*Be still, and know that I am God . . .*' Psalm 42:9–11 has these words, which expressed something both of my pain and yet my desire to hold on to God:

> *I say to God my Rock,*
> '*Why have you forgotten me?*
> *Why must I go about mourning,*
> *oppressed by the enemy?*'
> [10] *My bones suffer mortal agony*
> *as my foes taunt me,*
> *saying to me all day long,*
> '*Where is your God?*'
> [11] *Why, my soul, are you downcast?*
> *Why so disturbed within me?*
> *Put your hope in God,*
> *for I will yet praise him,*
> *my Saviour and my God.*

My turning point was a trip to Israel in 2006 when a couple invited me to join a pilgrimage there. It was three years on from my husband's death and my prayer life and Bible reading seemed purposeless. One evening the Garden of Gethsemane was opened especially for our group to reflect and pray.

Our immediate surroundings were so quiet, just the smell of the olive trees, and yet below us was the noise of the busy bus station as the world travelled on. As I sat on a stone, hope was born. I could hear in my head Jesus praying '*not my will, but yours be done*'¹⁵ and that became my prayer then, as it has since. Not that I am always sure what his will is for me. I've just had a milestone birthday and wonder what else he has in store for me: I find that both daunting and exciting.

I still see my precious husband living on in so many ways. On one occasion our daughter was holding forth about a burning topical social issue at the meal table when we had a family gathering, and when she stopped my son-in-law just said, 'Thank you, Dad.' My grandson was born a few months after my husband died so he knew our daughter was pregnant but never got to see his grandson. But that has made him very special and he always refers to my husband as 'the grandad I never knew'. My husband had longed for one of the family to be a sports enthusiast – he eventually got one even though he never met him. I only have to look at the eyes of my family to see him – blue bright eyes right down to my great-granddaughter. I thank Jesus for all my family with all the complexities of family life but with all the love too.

Both these losses have been a long path to travel: but hope and joy have been and are there too. Above all, I do know that even when I'm not aware of it, Jesus is walking with me and we will get to Emmaus and one day eat together in his kingdom.

Final Reflections

So you have persisted this far (unless you are one of those peo-ple who turns to the back of any book first!). Here are some final reflections before you go.

First of all, I believe that God honours, and knows, all of our stories. Travelling in France one year I visited some of the many cemeteries with war graves. I was struck by the number of graves where the names of the servicemen buried there were not known, but on each one it said 'Known unto God'. The stories that we have looked at in this book, and others, remind us that no story is lost to God, even though the names might be unknown to other people.

Secondly, *your* particular story is important. You may not feel it – at times you may feel as if somehow your story, or even you yourself, have got lost. You may feel unimportant, as most of us do at least some of the time, as though you don't matter. However, the biblical story is one that tells us that every individual is of huge importance to God – more precious than sparrows, as Jesus puts it, and with every hair on our heads numbered.[1]

Thirdly, these stories remind us that God can step into our story – or perhaps more accurately, we can see where he is in our story – at any time. He may do so in a myriad of ways. Often this is through each other, as others in our lives are 'God with skin on'[2] to us, expressing his love, forgiveness and welcome. Sometimes we experience God with us through reading the Bible, or through something we see, hear or experience. The encounter with the man at the pool of Bethesda reminds us that the initiative is always God's, but we may need to take a step too.

Linked with this idea of God stepping into our story is the important truth that God, as the master story-teller, can write a different story for us (perhaps more accurately, with us), better than the one we imagined or were writing without reference to him. When we look ahead we can write ourselves a fearful story, but God can come with another thread where, perhaps like the dying thief, we find peace, even amid the uncertainty, as we hear Jesus' promise to us. We can write a story where we remain imprisoned by shame, but both the woman who encounters Jesus after adultery and the one who anoints his feet remind us that Jesus sees us with mercy and offers a new start. The road to Emmaus shows us that even in times of great pain, God walks with us and can bring comfort and even, in time, joy.

In a wider context, God is telling an extraordinary story, which spans every decade, every millennia. It is the story which began before creation, a story which saw Jesus stretch out his arms in welcome on the cross, a story which will continue into a time when '*God's dwelling-place is . . . among the people, and he will dwell with them. They will be his people, and God himself will be with them and be their God*', when '*He will wipe every tear from their eyes*' when '"*There will be no more death" or mourning or crying or pain, for the old order of things has passed away*'.[3] He invites us to be part of history – his story – through friendship with him. The story God can write both in and through us is one that makes us more human, not less,[4] which can open us up to new possibilities through discovering a God who loves us with what Brennan Manning calls 'relentless tenderness'.[5]

If you would like to share your story, I would love to hear it, whether you are just exploring faith, or have been on that journey a long time – I can be contacted via www.jeanniekendall. co.uk. Above all, I hope that these stories will help you know more than you did before that you are infinitely precious to God.

Can a mother forget the infant at her breast,
walk away from the baby she bore?
But even if mothers forget,
I'd never forget you – never.
Look, I've written your names on the backs of my hands.[6]

Acknowledgements

To be honest, before writing this book I never read the acknowledgements (and only sometimes the dedications). Entering the new, mysterious world of publishing has given me a new fascination with them. So if you as a reader got this far, thank you!

As the TV says, in no particular order, apart from the last two paragraphs . . .

I want to thank the whole team at Authentic, who have steered me through the maze to get this far, and who believed in the book. Your encouragement has been so important. Thank you so much Donna, Becky, Rachael, Charlie and my editor, Sheila. You have all been such a help and encouragement in the birth of this book.

To those of you who read early chapters and gave comment – the positive and not-so-positive were equally helpful in shaping the result.

Thank you to all those who took time to read the book amid your busy lives and write an endorsement. Your willingness to do that means a great deal.

Particular thanks to Paul Goodliff, who has known me a long time, not just for writing the Foreword, but also for many times when, way back, we were at the same church and you ministered to me. You once brought a promise that God would take the broken and stony parts of my heart and turn them to warm flesh. I hope you can see this book as evidence of that.

A special thank you goes to Rachel Johnson (Doctor Rachel!) who tirelessly read the first drafts, changing dashes to commas and spending time with me to help me grapple with referencing. I still don't understand a 'hanging this', mind you. You are my longest-standing friend and you have been a star.

To Colin and Lorri Dawson, who put me in contact with Peter and Jackie Townsend, who allowed me access to their retreat for the undisturbed, concentrated writing which was so essential at that part of the process.

My thanks to all those writers, speakers, counsellors and friends who have contributed to my still so limited understanding of both myself and God. You too are unnamed, but known to God. You have my gratitude.

The churches that I have been part of each have a place in my heart: St Martin and St Meriadoc Camborne where I first came to faith in the time of Basil Brown and Barry Kissell, Streatham Baptist Church where I worshipped for thirty-eight years and worked for twenty-eight, and Carshalton Beeches Baptist where I am now. Particular thanks go to the Beeches church family for giving me the sabbatical without which this book would never have been completed, and for all your support in so many ways. I want to pay particular tribute to my colleague Phil whose response to me talking about writing a book was an encouraging, unsurprised 'well, yes' and who has been a huge joy to minister with and a personal support in many ways through the last eight years. I have learned such a lot from you.

To all of you who let me tell your stories – I know you appear in the dedication, but again here I want to say how brave you have been. Sometimes I have cried as I listened or wrote, but I know that God is so proud of you and will use your stories to help others. Some of you I already knew, some of you it has been humbling and delightful to get to know.

To my precious family: Malc, your support for this book from that first day in Jersey has been tireless. You've made tea, reminded me why I am doing this, been a sounding board, and are my life's companion. God knew what he was doing that holiday in Salcombe. Amy and Ross, our precious children, holding you from birth and watching you grow has reminded me again and again of God's love for us, so much more faithful and powerful than mine for you. My story has been enriched by watching you become the people you are, and seeing Vali and Helen become part of your and our lives. Our amazing grandchildren, Faith and Gabriel – you keep Nana smiling and I can't wait to watch your story unfold further. I hope all of you can look past my frailties and failings and see Jesus. He's been my closest friend and I want him to be yours too.

Finally, dear Jesus. You took this broken, fearful teenager and turned her life upside down. What a journey so far . . . it really is all about you, your endless love and compassion. Please take these inadequate words and use them to help people see how amazing you are, and your love for them . . .

Notes

Introduction

[1] Nigel Wright, *The Real Godsend* (Abingdon: Bible Reading Fellowship, 2009), p. 97. Used with permission.

1 Leaving Home

[1] Leviticus 19:33,34.
[2] For further information see http://www.searo.who.int/entity/leprosy/topics/the_disease https://www.lepra.org.uk/ and https://www.leprosymission.org/ (all accessed 23.7.18).
[3] The word literally means 'mouthpiece'.
[4] See for example 1 Kings 18.
[5] E.g. Restoring the spring recorded in 2 Kings 2:19–22, the miraculous provision of oil for a needy family found in 2 Kings 4:1–7, and the birth of a child to a barren woman and later his raising the child to life from 2 Kings 4:8–37.
[6] We can assume from the story that at this point the two nations are not actively at war, though the king of Israel's later response makes clear there is still tension and uncertainty.
[7] 2 Kings 5:5,6.
[8] Sometimes shortened to Joram. He was king of the northern kingdom, where Elisha lived, but there was also a king of Judah with the same name, who was his brother-in-law.

9 In contrast to another maid, Rhoda, who is mentioned in Acts 12:12–15.
10 See Matthew 2:13–15,19–23.
11 For details of the organisation see http://relief.medair.org (accessed 23.7.18).
12 For more details about this practice, usually abbreviated to FGM, and an organisation seeking to end it, see https://www.28toomany .org (accessed 23.7.18). See also Elaine Storkey, *Scars Across Humanity* (London: SPCK, 2015).

2 Living with Depression

1 From *THE PROBLEM OF PAIN* by CS Lewis © copyright CS Lewis Pte Ltd 1940 (London: HarperCollins, 2012 edition), p. 161.
2 There are various ways to classify the Psalms. Anderson suggests The Praises of God (general, kingship or songs of Zion), Declarative Praises of the Individual, Declarative Praises of the People, Individual Laments (for the unjustly accused or of penitence), Laments of the Nation, Psalms of Confidence, Royal Psalms and Minor Types. A.A. Anderson, *The Book of Psalms* (London: Marshall, Morgan & Scott, 1972), pp. 31–32.
3 Others include Psalm 3, 5, 6, 7, 17, 22, 25, 26, 27, 28, 35, 39, 41, 42–3 (probably originally one psalm), 51, 54, 55, 56, 57, 59, 61, 63, 64, 69, 86, 88, 102, 109, 130, 140, 141 and 143.
4 See for example Job 11:10–16; 19:13–21.
5 Psalm 88:18.
6 See http://www.online-literature.com/hans_christian_andersen/ 981 (accessed 11.6.18).
7 Isaiah 45:3, NRSV.

3 Searching for Meaning

1 Ecclesiastes 1:2.
2 Matthew 2:8.

3 Richard Slater, 1854–1939, https://www.hymnsandcarolsof-christmas.com/Hymns_and_Carols/when_wise_men_came_seeking.htm (accessed 13.9.18).

4 When the dating of Jesus' birth was set by the monk Dionysius the Small in AD525 at the request of Pope John 1, an error was made.

5 Genesis 35:19,20.

6 The link with kings may originate from Psalm 72:10: '*May the kings of Tarshish and of distant shores bring tribute to him. May the kings of Sheba and Seba present him with gifts.*' This psalm is originally about King Solomon. The tradition of them as kings dates back to the second century theologian Tertullian.

7 For more detail see Paul Beasley-Murray, *Joy to the World: Preaching the Christmas Story* (Nottingham: IVP, 2005), p. 38.

8 If this thought is new to you, do read Romans 8:18–21 and Colossians 1:15–20.

9 See Daniel 1:20; 2:2; 4:7; 5:7.

10 Including Haley's comet which appeared in 11BC or a conjunction of Jupiter, Venus and Saturn in 7BC. This is perhaps most likely both in timing and as Jupiter was seen as the royal planet. However, we cannot be certain.

11 See for example Michael Green, *The Message of Matthew* (Leicester: IVP, 1988), p. 68.

12 Put simply, that there is one reality, and God is the universe, or that God is part of nature and not distinct from it.

13 Revelation 21:1.

14 Psalm 19:1.

15 See John 1:3; Colossians 1:16.

16 For just one example, see Joyce Huggett's classic book *Listening to God* (London: Hodder & Stoughton, 2016), pp. 96–104.

17 He was half-Jew, half-Edomite, i.e. from the people group descended from Esau, not (as the Jews) from Jacob. The two groups were rivals despite their close ethnic relationship. He was born in 73BC and named king by the Roman Senate in 40BC.

18 Jews and other Semitic people do not eat pork. Herod was an Edomite – i.e. descended from Esau. Cited in Beasley-Murray, *Joy to the World*, p. 55.

[19] This is recorded by the Jewish historian Josephus. Josephus, *Antiquities*, 17.6.174–175 and in other places such as Green, *The Message of Matthew*, p. 71 and John MacArthur, *Acts 1–12* (Chicago, IL: Moody Bible Institute, 1994), p. 320.

[20] See 1 Samuel 16:1; 17:12; 2 Samuel 23:14,15.

[21] See Matthew 2:13–18 and chapter 6 of this book.

[22] Numbers 24:17.

[23] Luke 2:1–20.

[24] Mark 4:35–41.

4 The Impact of Forgiveness

[1] Colossians 3:12,13, MSG.

[2] Mark 2:5.

[3] Mark 2:8–10.

[4] Mark 2:11.

[5] The Gospel of Mark is generally thought to have been written by John Mark, who is mentioned in the Acts of the Apostles, drawing on the memories of Peter the apostle. The same story is told in Matthew 9:1–8 and Luke 5:18–26.

[6] See Tom Wright, *Mark for Everyone* (London: SPCK, 2001), p. 16. Alternatively it could have been Peter and Andrew's house, which it is clear he used – see Mark 1:29–31.

[7] See for example Job 4:7 and the general argument of Job's friends. See also chapter 8 of this book. That sickness was caused by sin was taught by many rabbis at the time.

[8] John 9:3.

[9] This situation is possible – conversion disorder, as it is called, can cause genuine physical symptoms which have a root psychological cause. It was the starting point for Freud's work.

[10] For example see Psalm 103:3–5 and Isaiah 43:25. It was not thought that even the Messiah would be able to forgive sins.

[11] See Leviticus 24:16; John 8:59.

[12] I'm not here saying they are separate – they are of course inextricably linked. We are whole people, every area of our lives affecting each

other. In the first few chapters of Mark's gospel alone Jesus shows his authority in his teaching (Mark 1:27), over sickness (Mark 3:1–6 among many examples), over the natural world (Mark 4:35–41), over demonic powers (Mark 5:1–20) and over death (Mark 5:21–43).

[13] In Mark's gospel, despite a prior Sabbath healing in 1:21–28, this is the first obvious conflict with the authorities and the first of five stories in 2:1 – 3:6 demonstrating growing opposition to Jesus.

[14] There are numerous examples: the title is used of Jesus eighty-one times in the Gospels. See Mark 8:31, 10:33, and notably at his trial, Mark 14:62. Jesus brought a new meaning to this title, involving suffering. See Walter Wessel, *Expositor's Bible Commentary: Mark* (Grand Rapids, MI: Zondervan, 1995), pp. 94–96.

[15] For example Tobias Hägerland, *Jesus and the Forgiveness of Sins: An Aspect of His Prophetic Mission* (Cambridge: Cambridge University Press, 2011), and Desmond M. Tutu and Revd. Mpho Tutu, *The Book of Forgiving: The Fourfold Path for Healing Ourselves and Our World* (London: HarperCollins, 2015).

[16] As a small number of examples for the many possibilities, see Matthew 6:14,15; Luke 6:37,38; Matthew 18:21–35.

[17] Luke 11:4.

[18] Luke 23:34.

[19] See also chapter 9 of this book.

5 Discovering Love

[1] 1 John 4:8.

[2] Jesus is the English version of the Greek Iēsous – the Hebrew-Aramaic original is Yeshu'a – a shortened version of yehōshu'a – Joshua.

[3] The first five books of the Bible.

[4] See John 3:1–21; 7:50,51; 19:39–42.

[5] Vv. 44–46.

[6] Matthew 26:6–13; Mark 14:3–9; John 12:1–11.

[7] It is sad that often people feel they have to wear a mask in church to be accepted, increasing the sense of isolation some people feel.

See Claire Musters' book *Taking Off the Mask* (Milton Keynes: Authentic Media, 2017) for a helpful exploration of some of the reasons for this.

8   Alcoholics Anonymous. See https://www.alcoholics-anonymous .org.uk (accessed 23.7.18).

6 Losing a Child

1   Dwight D. Eisenhower Quotes (nd). https://www.brainyquote .com/quotes/dwight_d_eisenhower_162228 (accessed 1.8.18).

2   I have not dealt in this chapter with the escape of Jesus' family to Egypt. Whilst highly significant, it is not part of the story of the massacre in Bethlehem as they have already left the area.

3   The Feast of the Holy Innocents, in the Western churches 28 December and in the Eastern churches, various dates.

4   From 'O Little Town of Bethlehem' by Phillips Brook (1835–93).

5   For example as pointed out (and contested) by D.A. Carson, *The Expositor's Bible Commentary: Matthew* (Grand Rapids, MI: Zondervan, 1995), pp. 93–94.

6   As well as the reference to Jeremiah, there are similarities with the ethnic cleansing by Pharaoh prior to the Exodus from which Moses escaped as a baby (Exodus 1:1 – 2:10).

7   See Beasley-Murray, *Joy to the World*, pp. 55–56 and Green, *The Message of Matthew*, pp. 71–72.

8   This was dealt with more fully in chapter 3 of this book.

9   Jeremiah 31:15.

10   Genesis 35:16–20.

11   Genesis 4.

12   2 Samuel 21:1–14.

13   Luke 2:35.

14   Jeremiah 31:16,17.

15   See Matthew 1:23.

16   This theme of God hearing and seeing the suffering runs right through the Bible. One example includes Exodus 3:7: '*The* LORD *said, "I have indeed seen the misery of my people . . . I have heard*

them crying out . . . and I am concerned about their suffering."' The shortest verse in the English translation of the Bible is, of course, the response of Jesus to the death of his friend Lazarus and the grief of Lazarus' sisters Mary and Martha: *'Jesus wept'* (John 11:35).

7 Overcoming Shame

1 After Luke 21:38. See for example Leon Morris, *The Gospel according to John* (London: Marshall, Morgan & Scott, 1972).
2 For example Mark 11:27–33.
3 Tom Wright, *John for Everyone Part 1* (London and Louisville, KY: SPCK and Westminster John Knox Press, 2004), pp. 111 ff.
4 Philippians 2:6, MSG.

8 Facing Long-term Illness

1 Joseph Conrad, *Lord Jim*, edited and Introduction by Allan Simmons (London: Penguin, 2007), p. 16.
2 Some translations add a footnote, such as this one in the NIV, including vv. 3b–4: *'paralysed – and they waited for the moving of the waters. ⁴ From time to time an angel of the Lord would come down and stir up the waters. The first one into the pool after each such disturbance would be cured of whatever disease they had.'* These are not in the most reliable manuscripts and seem to be a helpful addition for later readers who would not have known the background.
3 A site which corresponds to this description has been excavated and can still be seen today.
4 E.g. John 3:5; 4:4–14; 7:37–39.
5 Tom Wright suggests it was at one stage dedicated to the healing god Asclepius, Tom Wright, *John for Everyone Part 1*, p. 55.
6 See John 9:1–3.
7 For example Leon Morris, *The Gospel according to John* (London: Marshall, Morgan & Scott, 1972), p. 306.

[8] See for example Mark 1:45; Luke 7:17; Luke 18:43.
[9] Such as Bruce Milne, *The Message of John* (Nottingham: IVP, 1993), p. 95.
[10] See William Barclay, *The Gospel of John Vol 1* (Edinburgh: Saint Andrew Press, 1956), p. 176.
[11] Sometimes called chronic fatigue syndrome.

9 Surviving Abuse

[1] Used with permission.
[2] Judges 21:25. I am reminded of the disturbing novel by William Golding, *Lord of the Flies* (First published London: Faber & Faber, 1954), where a group of schoolboys are marooned on an island. Deprived of external constraints, initial organisation gives way to chaos and destruction, leading to the murder of one of the boys.
[3] The writer of Judges makes no negative comment about him having a concubine, so we must assume this was allowed for Levites. However, it is the only biblical mention of Levites and concubines, and of course the story has a disastrous outcome.
[4] In the original Hebrew.
[5] See Genesis 18 – 19, with the direct parallel in 19:5 ff.
[6] He later says, in Judges 20:5, 'They raped my concubine, and she died' but he may have been simply covering for his own neglect. Chapter 20 makes clear that at no point does he take responsibility for what happened to her.
[7] See for example 1 Samuel 11:7.
[8] See Phyllis Trible, *Texts of Terror* (London: SCM Press, 2002), pp. 64–65.

10 Confronting Death

[1] John 11:25,26.
[2] Across the four gospels: Luke 23:34; Luke 23:43; John 19:26,27; Matthew 27:46/Mark 15:34; John 19:28; John 19:30; Luke 23:46.

³ See John 19:31–33. The soldiers broke the legs of the two thieves with Jesus to hasten their deaths, but Jesus was already dead.

⁴ Some have argued that Jesus died of heart failure. For a helpful scientific perspective see https://www.theguardian.com/science/2004/apr/08/thisweekssciencequestions (accessed 7.9.18).

⁵ Matthew 27:38.

⁶ John 19:41.

⁷ https://www.mndassociation.org/wp-content/uploads/mnd-association-key-messages-infographic.pdf (accessed 14.6.18).

11 Finding Hope

¹ 1 Peter 1:3.

² *'My God, my God, why have you forsaken me?'* from Psalm 22:1.

³ Some commentators, such as Norval Geldenhuys, *Commentary on the Gospel of Luke* in the New London Commentary series (London: Marshall, Morgan & Scott, 1950), pp. 631–642; and Darrell Bock, *Luke* in the *NIV Application Commentary* series (Grand Rapids, MI: Zondervan, 1998), p. 612, assume two men, but I think a couple make more sense of the hospitality they offer. The wife of 'Clopas' is mentioned as being present at the cross in John 19:25, but even if they were husband and wife we cannot be sure if she is the same woman mentioned in John, and she is not named in this story, so falls within the remit of this book. In imagining her at the crucifixion I am not assuming she is Mary, Clopas' wife.

⁴ See John 20:19: *'On the evening of that first day of the week, when the disciples were together, with the doors locked for fear of the Jewish leaders . . .'*

⁵ Such as Isaiah 53.

⁶ E.g. Mary in the garden, John 20:15 or the disciples fishing, John 21:4. Most resurrection stories appear in the gospels but there is also a short list of appearances in 1 Corinthians 15:5–8.

⁷ Emmaus was west of Jerusalem.

⁸ As James 3:1 reminds us.

⁹ Genesis 3:7.

[10] Barbara Brown Taylor, *Home by Another Way: Biblical Meditations Through the Christian Year* (London: SPCK, 2011), pp. 119–123.

[11] A phrase I first heard in a sermon by Revd. Nigel Wright in Spurgeon's College chapel, I think in 2002.

[12] 2 Corinthians 1:3,4.

[13] 2 Samuel 18:19 – 19:4.

[14] Deuteronomy 33:25, ESV.

[15] Luke 22:42.

Final Reflections

[1] Matthew 10:30,31.

[2] I have been using this phrase for many years and had always assumed it was original. I have since heard it used elsewhere, but no one appears to know its origin.

[3] Revelation 21:3,4.

[4] For a wonderful exploration of this idea, see Joe Haward's masterful book, *The Ghost of Perfection* (Eugene, OR: Resource Publications, 2017).

[5] Brennan Manning, *The Relentless Tenderness of Jesus* (Grand Rapids, MI: Fleming H. Revell, 2004). Used with permission.

[6] Isaiah 49:15,16, MSG.

Bibliography

Anderson, A.A., *The Book of Psalms* (London: Marshall, Morgan & Scott, 1972).

Andersen, Hans, *His Classic Fairy Tales* (trans. Erik Haugaard; London: Book Club Associates, 1977).

Barclay, William, *The Gospel of John Vol 1* (Edinburgh: Saint Andrew Press, 1956).

Beasley-Murray, Paul, *Joy to the World: Preaching the Christmas Story* (Nottingham: IVP, 2005).

Bock, Darrell, *Luke: The NIV Application Commentary from Biblical Text to Contemporary Life* (Grand Rapids, MI: Zondervan, 1996).

Brown Taylor, Barbara, *Home by Another Way* (London: SPCK, 2011).

Carson, D.A., *The Expositor's Bible Commentary: Matthew* (Grand Rapids, MI: Zondervan, 1995).

Conrad, Joseph, *Lord Jim*, edited and Introduction by Allan Simmons (London: Penguin, 2007).

Geldenhuys, Norval, *Commentary on the Gospel of Luke.* New London Commentary series (London: Marshall, Morgan & Scott, 1950).

Golding, William, *Lord of the Flies* (London: Faber & Faber, 1954).

Green, Michael, *The Message of Matthew* (Nottingham: IVP, 2000).

Hägerland, Tobias, *Jesus and the Forgiveness of Sins: An Aspect of His Prophetic Mission* (Cambridge: Cambridge University Press, 2011).

Haward, Joe, *The Ghost of Perfection* (Eugene, OR: Resource Publications, 2017).

Huggett, Joyce, *Listening to God* (London: Hodder & Stoughton, 2016).

Josephus, *Antiquities.*

Lewis, CS, *The Problem of Pain.* CS Lewis Signature Classics Edition (London: HarperCollins, 2012).

MacArthur, John, *Acts 1–12* (Chicago, IL: Moody Bible Institute, 1994).

Manning, Brennan, *The Relentless Tenderness of Jesus* (Grand Rapids, MI: Fleming H. Revell, 2004).

Milne, Bruce, *The Message of John* (Nottingham: IVP, 1993).

Morris, Leon, *The Gospel according to John* (London: Marshall, Morgan & Scott, 1971).

Musters, Claire, *Taking Off the Mask* (Milton Keynes: Authentic Media, 2017).

Storkey, Elaine, *Scars Across Humanity* (London: SPCK, 2015).

Trible, Phyllis, *Texts of Terror* (London: SCM Press, 2002).

Tutu, Desmond M. and Revd. Mpho Tutu, *The Book of Forgiving: The Fourfold Path for Healing Ourselves and Our World* (London: HarperCollins, 2015).

Wessel, Walter, *Expositor's Bible Commentary: Mark* (Grand Rapids, MI: Zondervan, 1995).

Wright, Nigel, *The Real Godsend* (Abingdon: Bible Reading Fellowship, 2009).

Wright, Tom, *John for Everyone Part 1* (London and Louisville, KY: SPCK and Westminster: John Knox Press, 2004).

Wright, Tom, *Mark for Everyone* (London: SPCK, 2001).

Websites

For further information see

https://www.28toomany.org

https://www.alcoholics-anonymous.org.uk

https://www.lepra.org.uk/ and https://www.leprosymission.org

https://www.mndassociation.org/wp-content/uploads/
mnd-association-key-messages-infographic.pdf

http://www.relief.medair.org

http://www.searo.who.int/entity/leprosy/topics/the_disease

https://www.theguardian.com/science/2004/apr/08/
thisweekssciencequestions

Scripture/Story Index

Judges 19	9	Surviving Abuse	The Levite's concubine
2 Kings 5:1–19	1	Leaving Home	A slave of Naaman's wife
Psalm 71	2	Living with Depression	An unknown psalm writer
Matthew 2:1–12	3	Searching for Meaning	The Magi
Matthew 2:13–18	6	Losing a Child	A mother of a baby boy killed by Herod's soldiers
Mark 2:1–12	4	The Impact of Forgiveness	A paralysed man
Luke 7:36–50	5	Discovering Love	A woman with a jar of perfume
Luke 23:32–43	10	Confronting Death	A criminal crucified beside Jesus
Luke 24:13–35	11	Finding Hope	A follower on the road to Emmaus
John 7:53 – 8:11	7	Overcoming Shame	A woman caught in adultery
John 5:1–15	8	Facing Long-term Illness	The invalid healed at the Pool of Bethesda

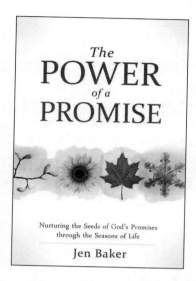

The Power of a Promise

Nurturing the seeds of God's promises through the seasons of life

Jen Baker

God loves to sow promises in our hearts, but they very rarely come to fruition immediately. Too often the storms of life can rob us of our hope, and we can give up on these promises. But what if these dark times were all part of the journey to fulfilled promises – would that give us hope to persevere?

Using a seed as a metaphor for the journey, Jen Baker shares six key stages a promise undergoes on its way to fulfilled purpose. Each stage of the journey is detailed, including what to expect and how we could respond.

Weaving together biblical reflections and real-life experiences, Jen inspires us to look at how we can all live fully in the calling God has uniquely designed for each of us.

978-1-78078-986-6

The Power of Seven

**49 devotional reflections,
7 biblical themes,
Genesis to Revelation**

Emily Owen

> *Why did I create sky?
> I created sky because I want you to reach.
> To reach for what I am offering you.
> To reach for me.*

Written in Emily Owen's unique, poetic style, this series of forty-nine devotions on seven biblical themes will inspire and gently steer you into a closer walk with Jesus.

Emily seamlessly weaves together reflections, prayers, personal stories and the encouraging 'voice' of God. Enjoy the world he gave you and stand together with him, with these seven themes as your guide: Creation, God *Is*, The Lord is My Shepherd, I AM, Echoes from the Cross, Add to Faith and Revelation Churches.

978-1-78078-990-3

Authentic

We trust you enjoyed reading this book
from Authentic. If you want to be
informed of any new titles from this author
and other releases you can sign up to the
Authentic newsletter by scanning below:

Online:
authenticmedia.co.uk

Follow us: